THE PO
OF LAW

# THE 1998
# Competition Act
# explained

## DAVID PICKERSGILL

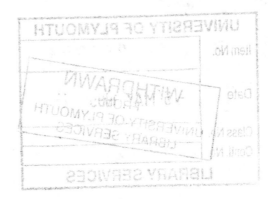

This book

CHARG

London: The Stationery Office

A CIP catalogue record for this book is available from the British Library
A Library of Congress CIP catalogue record has been applied for

First published 1999

ISBN 0 11 702683 2

Printed in the United Kingdom for the Stationery Office by Albert Gait Ltd, Grimsby
J69817 C10 3/99 9385 9688

The *Guide to the Competition Act* was written by David Pickersgill, a practising barrister at Bell Yard Chambers, 116–118 Chancery Lane, London WC2A 1PP.
Telephone: 0171 306 9292
Fax: 0171 404 5143

## *Disclaimer*

This publication is intended to be a brief commentary on the Competition Act and should not be relied upon by any party without taking further legal advice.

Contents

## CHAPTER II ABUSE OF DOMINANT POSITION

*Introduction*

*The prohibition*

*Excluded cases*

*Notification*

## CHAPTER III INVESTIGATION AND ENFORCEMENT

*Investigations*

*Enforcement*

**CHAPTER IV THE COMPETITION COMMISSION AND APPEALS**

*The Commission*

**CHAPTER V MISCELLANEOUS**

*Vertical agreements and land agreements*

*Director's rules, guidance and fees*

*Regulators*

**SCHEDULES:**

## INTRODUCTION

The Competition Act 1998 is introduced following widespread dissatisfaction that had developed in relation to competition law in the United Kingdom. The Government have responded by establishing new legislation which is closely based on the current legal regime operating within the European Community. The Government's objective is reform that achieves uniformity and consistency which will assist the business community and the consumer. Accordingly, interpretation of the new Act will be based on European Community law.

The new Act will relate directly to trade within the United Kingdom whilst EC competition law will continue to concern itself with trade between member states of the Community.

In harmony with the EC Treaty the new Act introduces a prohibition-based approach to anti-competitive behaviour. The first prohibition is called the 'Chapter I Prohibition' and is closely based on Article 85 of the EC Treaty. It specifically deals with anti-competitive agreements, concerted practises and the operation of cartels.

The second prohibition is called the 'Chapter II prohibition' and it is closely based on Article 86 of the EC Treaty. It aims at preventing abusive, anti-competitive conduct in the market place.

### *Reform*

The prohibitions contained within the new Act replace the Restrictive Trade Practises Act 1976, the Resale Prices Act 1976, the majority of the Competition Act 1980 and related provisions in other legislation.

### *Enforcement*

The new regime will be enforced by the Director General of Fair Trading ("the Director").

The regulated utility Directors will exercise concurrent powers in their particular sectors.

### *Exemptions and Exclusions*

Certain agreements will be exempt from the Chapter I Prohibition if they meet the criteria established within the Act. Further, certain classes of agreements and conduct will be excluded from the effect of the prohibitions.

### *Guidance and Decisions*

The new Act sets out procedures whereby concerned parties can apply to the Director for guidance or a decision as to whether their agreements or conduct infringe the prohibitions.

### Directions made by the Director

Following a decision the Director may make a direction requiring a change or an end to the offending agreement or conduct. The Director may apply to a court for an order requiring the implementation of the directions.

### Penalties

The civil courts may impose penalties on offending parties. Small agreements and conduct of minor significance will be immune from such penalties.

### Investigations

The Director will have extensive powers of investigation. If he has reasonable grounds for suspecting an infringement of either prohibition he may;

-   require the production of documents;
-   require an explanation relating to documents;
-   enter premises to require the production or explanation of such documents;
-   enter premises with a warrant using such force as is reasonably necessary for the same purpose.

The Act also provides that the Director assists the competition authorities at the European Commission by conducting investigations into alleged breaches of EC competition law.

Further, powers to investigate monopolies are strengthened under the new Act.

### Obstruction and Non-compliance

A number of new criminal offences are created which apply to individuals who obstruct or do not comply with requirements of the Director when investigating an alleged infringement.

### Information

The Director is required to regularly publish information relating to the application and enforcement of the prohibitions.

Information which is obtained by the Director must be protected from misuse and wrongful disclosure.

### The Competition Commission

This new institution will have two functions. Firstly, it will act as an appeal tribunal for applications made by parties who wish to appeal against decisions made by the Director. Secondly, the functions of the Monopolies and Mergers Commission will transfer to the Competition Commission.

This plain guide has been written to assist in the reading of the new Act and the commentary should not be relied upon as legal authority.

# A Plain Guide to
# The Competition Act
# 1998

**1998 Chapter 41**

An Act to make provision about competition and the abuse of a dominant position in the market; to confer powers in relation to investigations conducted in connection with Article 85 or 86 of the treaty establishing the European Community; to amend the Fair Trading Act 1973 in relation to information which may be required in connection with investigations under that Act; to make provision with respect to the meaning of "supply of services" in the Fair Trading Act 1973; and for connected purposes.

[9th November 1998]

Be it enacted by the Queen's most Excellent Majesty, by and with the advice and consent of the Lords Spiritual and Temporal, and Commons, in this present Parliament assembled, and by the authority of the same, as follows:-

PART I COMPETITION

CHAPTER I AGREEMENTS

## Introduction

1.  The following shall cease to have effect-

    (a) the Restrictive Practices Court Act 1976 (c. 33),
    (b) the Restrictive Trade Practices Act 1976 (c. 34),
    (c) the Resale Prices Act 1976 (c. 53), and
    (d) the Restrictive Trade Practices Act 1977 (c. 19).

**Section 1**
*Section 1 repeals the previous legislation as listed at (a) to (d).*

## The prohibition

2.– (1) Subject to section 3, agreements between undertakings, decisions by associations of undertakings or concerted practices which-

    (a) may affect trade within the United Kingdom, and
    (b) have as their object or effect the prevention, restriction or distortion of competition within the United Kingdom,

are prohibited unless they are exempt in accordance with the provisions of this Part.

## Section 2 (1) THE CHAPTER I PROHIBITION

*The wording used in the Chapter I Prohibition is closely based on Article 85(1) of the EC Treaty.*

*The intention of the Government is that the competition authorities and the courts in the United Kingdom interpret competition legislation in harmony with European Community law. Therefore, for the purpose of interpretation we must look to the principles and decisions followed by the European Commission and the European Court of Justice.*

### 'agreements'

*For the purposes of the Chapter I Prohibition, the definition of 'agreement' is wide. The term encompasses informal verbal agreements as well as those in written form.*

*Therefore, S.2 (1) will include the 'gentleman's agreement' which may be merely an expression by persons of a joint intention to conduct themselves within a market in a specific way.*

### 'undertakings'

*This term includes all forms of commercial entreprise. Examples include:*

– *Corporations*

– *Partnerships*

– *Individuals*

– *'State' owned organisations.*

### 'decisions by associations of undertakings'

*The term 'associations of undertakings' means trade associations and organisations such as co-operatives.*

*The 'decision' by a trade association may be a formal agreement between the members. Alternatively, it may take the form of a non-binding recommendation made by the officers of the trade association to its members.*

### 'concerted practises'

*This wide reaching term is designed to target practises less easy to detect than the written agreement but which can prove just as damaging to the competitive market.*

*The European Court of Justice has defined 'concerted practise' as;*

*'a form of co-ordination between entreprises that has not yet reached the point where there is a contract in the true sense of the word but which, in practise, consciously substitutes a practical co-operation for the risks of competition.'[1]*

---

[1] *ICI v Commission (48/69) 1972 ECR 621.*

## Section 2 (1) (a)
*'may affect trade within the United Kingdom'*

### i. Jurisdiction
*This phrase expressly states the jurisdiction in which the Competition Act 1998 is intended to operate. If an agreement 'affects trade between Member States' of the European Community it will fall within the jurisdiction of EC competition law. If the agreement affects trade within the United Kingdom only the matter will fall within the jurisdiction of the Competition Act.*

### ii. Potential Effect
*The word 'may' indicates that agreements which potentially affect trade will be subject to the Chapter I Prohibition.*

### iii. Appreciable Effect
*In line with the principle followed in EC law, agreements that do not have an 'appreciable effect' on competition will not be subject to the Chapter I Prohibition.*

*The next question for some parties will centre on whether their agreements have such an effect.*

*A principal factor to consider relates to the combined market share of the parties. It is anticipated that where combined market share falls below 10%, the agreements would not have an appreciable affect on competition within the market.*

*Secondly, despite the fact that the agreement infringes the Chapter I Prohibition the undertakings may enjoy immunity since their combined turnover falls below a specified threshold. Further provisions under secondary legislation are expected to reveal the threshold figure.*

*Thirdly, other factors may be considered including;*

- *the nature of the agreement;*
- *the actual contents of the agreement;*
- *the structure of the market affected by the agreement.*

*It is important to view Section 40 of this Act which essentially replicates this principle.*

## Section 2 (1)(b)

### 'object'
*If an agreement has as its intention or purpose the prevention, restriction or distortion of competition it will infringe the Chapter I Prohibition.*

*The European Court of Justice has stated;*

*'...it is not necessary to take into consideration the actual effects of an agreement where its purpose is to prevent, restrict or distort competition.'[2]*

### 'effect'
*The competition authorities conduct an economic analysis in order to prove effect. However, the European Court of Justice has encouraged an analysis that balances identifiable anti-competitive effect against pro-competitive effect.*

*As stated above, in order to breach the Chapter I Prohibition the resulting effect on competition must be appreciable or significant.*

### Exemptions
*S. 2(1)(b) introduces provision that certain agreements will be exempt from the Chapter I Prohibition.*

*There are three types of exemption;*

— *the individual exemption ( see S.4 )*

— *the block exemption ( see S.6 )*

— *the parallel exemption ( see S.10 )*

[2] *Consten and Grundig v Commission (56 and 58/64) 1966 ECR 299*

(2) Subsection (1) applies, in particular, to agreements, decisions or practices which-

### Section 2 (2)
*This section provides a non-exhaustive list of examples of the kinds of agreements, decisions and practises that are prohibited.*

  (a) directly or indirectly fix purchase or selling prices or any other trading conditions;

## Section 2 (2)(a)

### Price fixing

*Agreements between undertakings to fix selling prices are strictly prohibited. This practise is a clear example of co-operation being pursued at the expense of the market's natural competitive forces. As the undertakings achieve secure prices and subsequent profits, the consumer is being deprived of the most competitive price and value.*

*Agreements that indirectly affect prices may be included in the category of price fixing. For example, collusion between undertakings with regard to discounts on sales or credit terms offered to customers.*

*Similarly, undertakings may agree to collude in relation to purchase prices. Clearly this practise eliminates the competitive nature of the market.*

### Fixing other trading conditions

*Rather than prices other trading conditions may be fixed in order to benefit the undertakings. For example, purchasers may collude as to which suppliers they will use and effectively control the structure of the market.*

*Under the category 'fixing other trading conditions' may fall the practise of 'bid-rigging'. This phrase refers to collusion by undertakings involved in the tendering process. Obviously any such collusion deprives the process of genuine competition.*

(b) limit or control production, markets, technical development or investment;

## Section 2 (2)(b)

### Limiting or controlling production, markets, technical development or investment

*Such practises may amount to the fixing of future price levels. Collusion between undertakings in relation to limiting the supply side of the market may have as its objective future price increases or the preservation of a price level.*

(c) share markets or sources of supply;

**Section 2 (2)(c)**

**Sharing markets**
*An example of market sharing may be found where undertakings agree to co-operate in relation to territory or volume of sales. Essentially, it allows the parties protection in their particular area of the market.*

(d) apply dissimilar conditions to equivalent transactions with other trading parties, thereby placing them at a competitive disadvantage;

**Section 2 (2)(d)**
*This sub-section refers to agreement with regard to differing conditions being applied to different parties although the transactions are essentially the same. For example, dominant undertakings may agree to offer discounts or rebates to certain customers but not to others. Naturally this form of agreement distorts the market and places competitors at a disadvantage.*

(e) make the conclusion of contracts subject to acceptance by the other parties of supplementary obligations which, by their nature or according to commercial usage, have no connection with the subject of such contracts.

**Section 2 (2)(e)**
*An example of point (e)occurs when a supplier of goods applies a condition that he will deal with the customer providing he purchases a supplementary product also. The customer may not require the supplementary product at all or require it at the supplier's price.*

(3) Subsection (1) applies only if the agreement, decision or practice is, or is intended to be, implemented in the United Kingdom.

(4) Any agreement or decision which is prohibited by subsection (1) is void.

(5) A provision of this Part which is expressed to apply to, or in relation to, an agreement is to be read as applying equally to, or in relation to, a decision by an association of undertakings or a concerted practice (but with any necessary modifications).

(6) Subsection (5) does not apply where the context otherwise requires.

(7) In this section "the United Kingdom" means, in relation to an agreement which operates or is intended to operate only in a part of the United Kingdom, that part.

(8) The prohibition imposed by subsection (1) is referred to in this Act as "the Chapter I prohibition".

**Excluded agreements**

**3.**– (1) The Chapter I prohibition does not apply in any of the cases in which it is excluded by or as a result of-

   (a) Schedule 1 (mergers and concentrations);
   (b) Schedule 2 (competition scrutiny under other enactments);
   (c) Schedule 3 (planning obligations and other general exclusions); or
   (d) Schedule 4 (professional rules).

**Section 3 (1)**
*This section introduces the four Schedules which contain categories of agreement that will be excluded from the Chapter I Prohibition.*

*Schedule 1 relates to agreements that result in mergers and concentrations and are subject to the Fair Trading Act 1973.*

*Schedule 2 refers to agreements which are subject to scrutiny under other competition legislation;*

– *the Financial Services Act 1986*

– *the Companies Act 1989*

– *the Broadcasting Act 1990*

– *the Environmental Act 1995.*

*Schedule 3 sets out general exclusions covering agreements that;*

– *are required to comply with planning obligations*

– *fall under section 21(2) of the Restrictive Trade Practices Act 1976*

– *form the constitution of a market regulated by the European Economic Area*

– *relate to services of general economic interest*

– *are needed in order to comply with specific legal requirements*

– *avoid conflict with international obligations*

– *are subject to public policy*

– *fall within coal and steel product provisions (European Coal and Steel Community Treaty)*

> – *fall within agricultural product provisions in the Council Regulation (EEC) No. 26/62.*
>
> *Schedule 4 refers to rules regulating a professional service, for example regulations and codes of practice.*

(2) The Secretary of State may at any time by order amend Schedule 1, with respect to the Chapter I prohibition, by-

   (a) providing for one or more additional exclusions; or

   (b) amending or removing any provision (whether or not it has been added by an order under this subsection).

(3) The Secretary of State may at any time by order amend Schedule 3, with respect to the Chapter I prohibition, by-

   (a) providing for one or more additional exclusions; or

   (b) amending or removing any provision-

      (i)  added by an order under this subsection; or

      (ii) included in paragraph 1, 2, 8 or 9 of Schedule 3.

> **Section 3 (2) and (3)**
> *This section states the Secretary of State's powers in relation to adding to, amending or removing from the exclusions contained within Schedules 1 and 3.*

(4) The power under subsection (3) to provide for an additional exclusion may be exercised only if it appears to the Secretary of State that agreements which fall within the additional exclusion-

   (a) do not in general have an adverse effect on competition, or

   (b) are, in general, best considered under Chapter II or the Fair Trading Act 1973.

(5) An order under subsection (2)(a) or (3)(a) may include provision (similar to that made with respect to any other exclusion provided by the relevant Schedule) for the exclusion concerned to cease to apply to a particular agreement.

(6) Schedule 3 also gives the Secretary of State power to exclude agreements from the Chapter I prohibition in certain circumstances.

**Exemptions**

4.–(1)  The Director may grant an exemption from the Chapter I prohibition with respect to a particular agreement if-

(a) a request for an exemption has been made to him under section 14 by a party to the agreement; and

(b) the agreement is one to which section 9 applies.

**Section 4 (1)**
*This section introduces the notion of individual exemption from the Chapter I Prohibition. The criteria relating to the application for an individual exemption is set out at section 9.*

*The 'Director' refers to the Director General of Fair Trading.*

(2) An exemption granted under this section is referred to in this Part as an individual exemption.

(3) The exemption-

(a) may be granted subject to such conditions or obligations as the Director considers it appropriate to impose; and

(b) has effect for such period as the Director considers appropriate.

**Section 4 (3) (a)and (b)**
*The Director can impose conditions, obligations and a specified time period on granting an individual exemption.*

(4) That period must be specified in the grant of the exemption.

(5) An individual exemption may be granted so as to have effect from a date earlier than that on which it is granted.

(6) On an application made in such way as may be specified by rules under section 51, the Director may extend the period for which an exemption has effect; but, if the rules so provide, he may do so only in specified circumstances.

5.– (1) If the Director has reasonable grounds for believing that there has been a material change of circumstance since he granted an individual exemption, he may by notice in writing-

(a) cancel the exemption;

(b) vary or remove any condition or obligation; or

(c) impose one or more additional conditions or obligations.

**Section 5 (1) (a) to (c)**

*This section gives the Director powers to make changes to an individual exemption when he has reasonable grounds to believe that there has been a material change of circumstances since he granted the exemption. He may;*

– *cancel the exemption;*

– *vary or remove a condition or obligation;*

– *add to the conditions or obligations.*

*The Director need only have reasonable grounds for believing that such changes exist. He may form this opinion himself or he may act following a complaint by a third party.*

(2) If the Director has a reasonable suspicion that the information on which he based his decision to grant an individual exemption was incomplete, false or misleading in a material particular, he may by notice in writing take any of the steps mentioned in subsection (1).

**Section 5 (2)**

*Similarly, the Director may act as above where he has reasonable suspicion that information previously submitted was;*

– *incomplete;*

– *false; or*

– *misleading.*

(3) Breach of a condition has the effect of cancelling the exemption.

(4) Failure to comply with an obligation allows the Director, by notice in writing, to take any of the steps mentioned in subsection (1).

**Section 5 (3) and (4)**

*These sub-sections state the consequences of not complying with a condition or obligation imposed by the Director.*

(5) Any step taken by the Director under subsection (1), (2) or (4) has effect from such time as may be specified in the notice.

(6) If an exemption is cancelled under subsection (2) or (4), the date specified in the notice cancelling it may be earlier than the date on which the notice is given.

(7) The Director may act under subsection (1), (2) or (4) on his own initiative or on a complaint made by any person.

**6.–** (1) If agreements which fall within a particular category of agreement are, in the opinion of the Director, likely to be agreements to which section 9 applies, the Director may recommend that the Secretary of State make an order specifying that category for the purposes of this section.

(2) The Secretary of State may make an order ("a block exemption order") giving effect to such a recommendation-

(a) in the form in which the recommendation is made; or
(b) subject to such modifications as he considers appropriate.

(3) An agreement which falls within a category specified in a block exemption order is exempt from the Chapter I prohibition.

(4) An exemption under this section is referred to in this Part as a block exemption.

**Section 6 (1) – (4)**
*This section introduces the block exemptions which include categories of agreement that the Director specifies will not be caught by the Chapter I Prohibition. The Director makes a recommendation to the Secretary of State to make an order that creates the block exemption. It is not necessary to notify the Director of an agreement that falls within a block exemption.*

*The criteria followed for granting a block exemption is stated at section 9.*

(5) A block exemption order may impose conditions or obligations subject to which a block exemption is to have effect.

**Section 6 (5)**
*As with individual exemptions a block exemption may impose specified conditions or obligations upon the parties to an agreement.*

(6) A block exemption order may provide-

(a) that breach of a condition imposed by the order has the effect of cancelling the block exemption in respect of an agreement;

(b) that if there is a failure to comply with an obligation imposed by the order, the Director may, by notice in writing, cancel the block exemption in respect of the agreement;

(c) that if the Director considers that a particular agreement is not one to which section 9 applies, he may cancel the block exemption in respect of that agreement.

**Section 6 (6)**
*This sub-section states the consequences of non-compliance with the conditions or obligations.*

(7) A block exemption order may provide that the order is to cease to have effect at the end of a specified period.

**Section 6 (7)**
*The block exemption may be subject to a time limit.*

(8) In this section and section 7 "specified" means specified in a block exemption order.

7.– (1) A block exemption order may provide that a party to an agreement which-

(a) does not qualify for the block exemption created by the order, but
(b) satisfies specified criteria,

may notify the Director of the agreement for the purposes of subsection (2).

**Section 7 (1)**
*This section deals with agreements that do not qualify for a block exemption but will if certain 'specified criteria' is satisfied. The party can then notify the Director and may then be subject to the exemption.*

(2) An agreement which is notified under any provision included in a block exemption order by virtue of subsection (1) is to be treated, as from the end of the notice period, as falling within a category specified in a block exemption order unless the Director-

(a) is opposed to its being so treated; and

(b) gives notice in writing to the party concerned of his opposition before the end of that period.

**Section 7 (2)**
*Following on from Section 7(1) above. If the criteria has been satisfied and the party has notified the Director then the agreement will be treated as exempt unless the Director opposes it in writing within the notice period. Section 7(4) defines "notice period."*

(3) If the Director gives notice of his opposition under subsection (2), the notification under subsection (1) is to be treated as both notification under section 14 and as a request for an individual exemption made under subsection (3) of that section.

(4) In this section "notice period" means such period as may be specified with a view to giving the Director sufficient time to consider whether to oppose under subsection (2).

8.– (1) Before making a recommendation under section 6(1), the Director must-

(a) publish details of his proposed recommendation in such a way as he thinks most suitable for bringing it to the attention of those likely to be affected; and
(b) consider any representations about it which are made to him.

(2) If the Secretary of State proposes to give effect to such a recommendation subject to modifications, he must inform the Director of the proposed modifications and take into account any comments made by the Director.

(3) If, in the opinion of the Director, it is appropriate to vary or revoke a block exemption order he may make a recommendation to that effect to the Secretary of State.

(4) Subsection (1) also applies to any proposed recommendation under subsection (3).

(5) Before exercising his power to vary or revoke a block exemption order (in a case where there has been no recommendation under subsection (3)), the Secretary of State must-

(a) inform the Director of the proposed variation or revocation; and
(b) take into account any comments made by the Director.

(6) A block exemption order may provide for a block exemption to have effect from a date earlier than that on which the order is made.

**Section 8**
*This section sets out procedure in relation to block exemptions including the role of the Director General of Fair Trading and the Secretary of State.*

9.  This section applies to any agreement which-

   (a) contributes to-
      (i)  improving production or distribution, or
      (ii) promoting technical or economic progress,

while allowing consumers a fair share of the resulting benefit; but

   (b) does not-
      (i)  impose on the undertakings concerned restrictions which are not indispensable to the attainment of those objectives; or

      (ii) afford the undertakings concerned the possibility of eliminating competition in respect of a substantial part of the products in question.

**Section 9**
*This important section establishes the criteria for the grant of individual and block exemptions.*

**'contributes to improving production or distribution'**
*Often this will involve an agreement aimed at arrangements for future production or distribution. The competition authorities require improvements and consequently benefits that outweigh any detrimental effect on competition in the market. The authorities require the existence of objective and appreciable advantages.*

*For example, agreements between undertakings aimed at longer production runs or delivery runs may improve the efficiency of the market by lowering running costs. The benefits in terms of prices, services, ranges of product etc should subsequently pass to the customer.*

**'promoting technical or economic progress'**
*'Technical and economic progress' specifically refers to agreements that allow companies collectively to improve the efficiency of the market in which they operate. Individually, an undertaking may find achieving such progress difficult or impossible.*

**'allowing consumers a fair share of the resulting benefit'**
*Essentially, this requirement protects the interest of the consumer. The contracting parties may attain greater efficiency and lower running costs but this requirement ensures benefits subsequently pass to customers.*

**Section 9 (b) (i)**
*Essentially, the restriction on competition should not be more than is necessary to obtain the benefit in question.*

**Section 9 (b) (ii)**
*The parties to the agreement must be able to prove by way of a market analysis that competition will not be eliminated.*

**10.–** (1) An agreement is exempt from the Chapter I prohibition if it is exempt from the Community prohibition-

**Section 10**
*Section 10 introduces 'parallel exemptions' which are exemptions from the prohibition stated in Article 85 of the EC Treaty. In brief, section 10 states that agreements exempt under Article 85 are also exempt from the Chapter I Prohibition if they affect trade between member states.*

   (a) by virtue of a Regulation,

**Section 10 (1) (a)**

**'a Regulation'**
*The European Parliament acting jointly with the Council of the European Union and the European Commission make regulations that are legally binding and have general application.*

**'the Commission'**
*The European Commission based in Brussels.*

   (b) because it has been given exemption by the Commission, or
   (c) because it has been notified to the Commission under the appropriate opposition or objection procedure and-

(i) the time for opposing, or objecting to, the agreement has expired and the Commission has not opposed it; or

(ii) the Commission has opposed, or objected to, the agreement but has withdrawn its opposition or objection.

(2) An agreement is exempt from the Chapter I prohibition if it does not affect trade between Member States but otherwise falls within a category of agreement which is exempt from the Community prohibition by virtue of a Regulation.

(3) An exemption from the Chapter I prohibition under this section is referred to in this Part as a parallel exemption.

(4) A parallel exemption-

(a) takes effect on the date on which the relevant exemption from the Community prohibition takes effect or, in the case of a parallel exemption under subsection (2), would take effect if the agreement in question affected trade between Member States; and

(b) ceases to have effect-

(i) if the relevant exemption from the Community prohibition ceases to have effect; or

(ii) on being cancelled by virtue of subsection (5) or (7).

(5) In such circumstances and manner as may be specified in rules made under section 51, the Director may-

(a) impose conditions or obligations subject to which a parallel exemption is to have effect;

(b) vary or remove any such condition or obligation;

(c) impose one or more additional conditions or obligations;

(d) cancel the exemption.

**Section 10 (5)**
*Parallel exemptions may also require that undertakings fulfil specified conditions and obligations.*

(6) In such circumstances as may be specified in rules made under section 51, the date from which cancellation of an exemption is to take effect may be earlier than the date on which notice of cancellation is given.

(7) Breach of a condition imposed by the Director has the effect of cancelling the exemption.

(8) In exercising his powers under this section, the Director may require any person who is a party to the agreement in question to give him such information as he may require.

(9) For the purpose of this section references to an agreement being exempt from the Community prohibition are to be read as including references to the prohibition being inapplicable to the agreement by virtue of a Regulation or a decision by the Commission.

(10) In this section-

"the Community prohibition" means the prohibition contained in-

(a) paragraph 1 of Article 85;
(b) any corresponding provision replacing, or otherwise derived from, that provision;
(c) such other Regulation as the Secretary of State may by order specify; and

"Regulation" means a Regulation adopted by the Commission or by the Council.

(11) This section has effect in relation to the prohibition contained in paragraph 1 of Article 53 of the EEA Agreement (and the EFTA Surveillance Authority) as it has effect in relation to the Community prohibition (and the Commission) subject to any modifications which the Secretary of State may by order prescribe.

11.– (1) The fact that a ruling may be given by virtue of Article 88 of the Treaty on the question whether or not agreements of a particular kind are prohibited by Article 85 does not prevent such agreements from being subject to the Chapter I prohibition.

(2) But the Secretary of State may by regulations make such provision as he considers appropriate for the purpose of granting an exemption from the Chapter I prohibition, in prescribed circumstances, in respect of such agreements.

(3) An exemption from the Chapter I prohibition by virtue of regulations under this section is referred to in this Part as a section 11 exemption.

**Section 11**
*The Secretary of State may make regulations that exempt certain agreements which are subject to transitional provisions under the EC Treaty.*

**Notification**

12.– (1) Sections 13 and 14 provide for an agreement to be examined by the Director on the application of a party to the agreement who thinks that it may infringe the Chapter I prohibition.

(2) Schedule 5 provides for the procedure to be followed-

(a) by any person making such an application; and
(b) by the Director, in considering such an application.

(3) The Secretary of State may by regulations make provision as to the application of sections 13 to 16 and Schedule 5, with such modifications (if any) as may be prescribed, in cases where the Director-

(a) has given a direction withdrawing an exclusion; or

(b) is considering whether to give such a direction.

---

**Section 12**

*Section 12 introduces the notification procedure by which a party can request examination of an agreement by the Director in order to ascertain whether it infringes the Chapter I Prohibition. The necessary procedure is set out at Schedule 5.*

*The application form is called Form N and should be submitted to the Director based at;*

*The Office of Fair Trading*
*Field House*
*15-25 Bream's Buildings*
*London EC4A 1PR*
*Telephone 0171 211 8000*
*Fax 0171 211 8800.*

*Further, the section allows the Secretary of State to make modifications in relation to the application of sections 13 to 16 and Schedule 5 in certain circumstances.*

---

**13.–** (1) A party to an agreement who applies for the agreement to be examined under this section must-

(a) notify the Director of the agreement; and

(b) apply to him for guidance.

(2) On an application under this section, the Director may give the applicant guidance as to whether or not, in his view, the agreement is likely to infringe the Chapter I prohibition.

---

**Section 13**

*This section facilitates the process by which an undertaking concerned as to whether an agreement is lawful or not can seek guidance directly from the Director. Section 15 deals with the effect of guidance.*

---

(3) If the Director considers that the agreement is likely to infringe the prohibition if it is not exempt, his guidance may indicate-

(a) whether the agreement is likely to be exempt from the prohibition under-
    (i)  a block exemption;
    (ii) a parallel exemption; or
    (iii) a section 11 exemption; or
(b) whether he would be likely to grant the agreement an individual exemption if asked to do so.

**Section 13 (3)**
*The Director may indicate whether the agreement is likely to be exempt under any of the four categories;*

–   *a block exemption*

–   *a parallel exemption*

–   *a section 11 exemption*

–   *an individual exemption*

(4) If an agreement to which the prohibition applies has been notified to the Director under this section, no penalty is to be imposed under this Part in respect of any infringement of the prohibition by the agreement which occurs during the period-

(a) beginning with the date on which notification was given; and
(b) ending with such date as may be specified in a notice in writing given to the applicant by the Director when the application has been determined.

**Section 13 (4)**
*Between the date of notification and the date of the determination no penalty can be imposed by the Director for the infringement.*

(5) The date specified in a notice under subsection (4)(b) may not be earlier than the date on which the notice is given.

14.– (1) A party to an agreement who applies for the agreement to be examined under this section must-

(a) notify the Director of the agreement; and
(b) apply to him for a decision.

> **Section 14 (1)**
> *This section provides the process by which an undertaking can apply to the Director for 'a decision' as to whether an agreement infringes the Chapter I Prohibition. The Director may indicate whether the agreement falls within an exclusion or one of the exemptions (see under S.13 above).*

(2) On an application under this section, the Director may make a decision as to-

 (a) whether the Chapter I prohibition has been infringed; and
 (b) if it has not been infringed, whether that is because of the effect of an exclusion or because the agreement is exempt from the prohibition.

(3) If an agreement is notified to the Director under this section, the application may include a request for the agreement to which it relates to be granted an individual exemption.

(4) If an agreement to which the prohibition applies has been notified to the Director under this section, no penalty is to be imposed under this Part in respect of any infringement of the prohibition by the agreement which occurs during the period-

 (a) beginning with the date on which notification was given; and
 (b) ending with such date as may be specified in a notice in writing given to the applicant by the Director when the application has been determined.

> **Section 14 (4)**
> *As with an application for guidance, no penalty can be imposed between the date of notification and the date of determination.*

(5) The date specified in a notice under subsection (4)(b) may not be earlier than the date on which the notice is given.

15.– (1) This section applies to an agreement if the Director has determined an application under section 13 by giving guidance that-

 (a) the agreement is unlikely to infringe the Chapter I prohibition, regardless of whether or not it is exempt;
 (b) the agreement is likely to be exempt under-
  (i) a block exemption;
  (ii) a parallel exemption; or
  (iii) a section 11 exemption; or
 (c) he would be likely to grant the agreement an individual exemption if asked to do so.

**Section 15**
*The effect of guidance.*

(2) The Director is to take no further action under this Part with respect to an agreement to which this section applies, unless-

(a) he has reasonable grounds for believing that there has been a material change of circumstance since he gave his guidance;

(b) he has a reasonable suspicion that the information on which he based his guidance was incomplete, false or misleading in a material particular;

(c) one of the parties to the agreement applies to him for a decision under section 14 with respect to the agreement; or

(d) a complaint about the agreement has been made to him by a person who is not a party to the agreement.

**Section 15 (2)**
*Once the Director has given guidance under section 13 his powers are limited as to taking further action. He may do so under the four grounds listed above at S. 15 (2)(a)-(d).*

(3) No penalty may be imposed under this Part in respect of any infringement of the Chapter I prohibition by an agreement to which this section applies.

**Section 15 (3)**
*Once guidance has been given no penalty can be imposed subject to S. 15 (4) and (5).*

(4) But the Director may remove the immunity given by subsection (3) if-

(a) he takes action under this Part with respect to the agreement in one of the circumstances mentioned in subsection (2);

(b) he considers it likely that the agreement will infringe the prohibition; and

(c) he gives notice in writing to the party on whose application the guidance was given that he is removing the immunity as from the date specified in his notice.

> **Section 15 (4)**
> *The immunity with regard to fines may be lifted following further action under the reasons at (2)(a)-(d) and it is considered likely that the agreement will infringe the Chapter I Prohibition.*

(5) If the Director has a reasonable suspicion that information-

  (a) on which he based his guidance, and
  (b) which was provided to him by a party to the agreement,

was incomplete, false or misleading in a material particular, the date specified in a notice under subsection (4)(c) may be earlier than the date on which the notice is given.

> **Section 15 (5)**
> *The Director may also lift the immunity from fines to a date earlier than the notice date. He may do this when he has reasonable suspicion that a party has provided incomplete, false or misleading material.*

16.– (1) This section applies to an agreement if the Director has determined an application under section 14 by making a decision that the agreement has not infringed the Chapter I prohibition.

> **Section 16 (1)**
> *This section applies to the effect of a decision made by the Director. His powers are limited as to taking further action. He may do so under the grounds listed at S.16 (2)(a) and (b).*

(2) The Director is to take no further action under this Part with respect to the agreement unless-

  (a) he has reasonable grounds for believing that there has been a material change of circumstance since he gave his decision; or
  (b) he has a reasonable suspicion that the information on which he based his decision was incomplete, false or misleading in a material particular.

**Section 16 (2)**
*The immunity with regard to fines may be lifted following further action under (2)(a)*
*and (b) if the Director considers it likely that the agreement will infringe the Chapter*
*I Prohibition.*

(3) No penalty may be imposed under this Part in respect of any infringement of the Chapter I prohibition by an agreement to which this section applies.

(4) But the Director may remove the immunity given by subsection (3) if-

    (a) he takes action under this Part with respect to the agreement in one of the circumstances mentioned in subsection (2);

    (b) he considers that it is likely that the agreement will infringe the prohibition; and

    (c) he gives notice in writing to the party on whose application the decision was made that he is removing the immunity as from the date specified in his notice.

(5) If the Director has a reasonable suspicion that information-

    (a) on which he based his decision, and

    (b) which was provided to him by a party to the agreement,

was incomplete, false or misleading in a material particular, the date specified in a notice under subsection (4)(c) may be earlier than the date on which the notice is given.

**Section 16 (5)**
*The Director has the same power as at section 15(5). He may lift the immunity from*
*fines to a date earlier than the notice date when he has reasonable suspicion that a*
*party has provided incomplete, false or misleading information.*

CHAPTER II

ABUSE OF DOMINANT POSITION

**Introduction**

**17.** Sections 2 to 10 of the Competition Act 1980 (control of anti-competitive practices) shall cease to have effect.

## The prohibition

**18.–** (1) Subject to section 19, any conduct on the part of one or more undertakings which amounts to the abuse of a dominant position in a market is prohibited if it may affect trade within the United Kingdom.

---

**Section 18**

*The Chapter II Prohibition is closely based on Article 86 of the EC Treaty and interpretation must be in accordance with the principles and decisions of the European Commission and the European Court of Justice.*

**Section 18 (1)**

**'Abuse of a dominant position'**

*The Chapter II Prohibition contains two important elements that must be assessed by the Director in ascertaining whether there has been an infringement.*

*Firstly, whether the undertaking involved holds a dominant position.*

*Secondly, if the undertaking is dominant, whether or not it is abusing the position.*

**'dominant position'**

*The Director will consider the following factors;*

i.  *'the definition' of the market in which the undertaking is operating;*

ii.  *whether the undertaking is 'dominant' in the market; and*

iii.  *whether the conduct of the undertaking amounts to an abuse of its dominant position.*

**i. 'market definition'**

*It is necessary to ascertain exactly what market the undertaking is operating within. Two factors will be taken into account. Firstly, exactly what is perceived as the relevant product market. Secondly, the geographic market.*

*'the relevant product market'*

*In viewing the question of dominance, it is essential to ascertain exactly which products or services should be considered.*

*Firstly, the competition authorities will look closely at what choice of product is left to the consumer. Essentially, they will examine whether the consumer is offered a range and whether he can switch to an alternative product. If this is the case, the so-called 'substitute' products will be included in the definition of the relevant product market. The authorities have termed this factor 'demand-side substitution'.*

*Secondly, the authorities will look closely at whether competing undertakings can enter the particular market and offer alternative or similar products. This factor has been termed as 'supply-side substitution.'*

### 'geographic market'
*The factor to consider is whether suppliers in other areas can provide alternative or similar products and provide competition. If this is the case, those other areas may be considered as part of the geographical market. Therefore, the geographical market may include areas outside the United Kingdom.*

### ii. 'dominance'
*The principal issue in relation to dominance is the power of an undertaking to behave independently of its competitors, customers and its consumers.*

*This applies equally to suppliers and purchasers of goods and services. The dominant supplier may be able to set high prices and enjoy independence without effective restraint. Similarly, the dominant purchaser may demand lower prices from its suppliers because it is not subject to competition.*

*Therefore, an analysis of 'independence' is required. The authorities will view closely the existing competitors and the extent of their market share and power. Further, as stated above the analysis will involve viewing potential competitors and particularly whether they can effectively enter the market.*

### 'Market share'
*There is no set figure relating to market share. The actual share will only be considered as a feature of the undertaking's dominance since other characteristics need to be considered. For example, an undertaking that holds 40% of a market may nevertheless be subjected to fierce competition. Alternatively, due to the fragmented structure of a market an undertaking with a much lower market share may be able to exert dominance and act independently.*

### 'Market entry'
*This term relates to the existence of and factors affecting potential competitors. The authorities will examine whether competitors have proper access to the market without any barriers.*

### Other constraints
*Other factors will be considered which act to constrain the dominant undertaking.*

(2) Conduct may, in particular, constitute such an abuse if it consists in-

    (a) directly or indirectly imposing unfair purchase or selling prices or other unfair trading conditions;

(b) limiting production, markets or technical development to the prejudice of consumers;

(c) applying dissimilar conditions to equivalent transactions with other trading parties, thereby placing them at a competitive disadvantage;

(d) making the conclusion of contracts subject to acceptance by the other parties of supplementary obligations which, by their nature or according to commercial usage, have no connection with the subject of the contracts.

## Section 18 (2) (a) to (d)

### iii. Conduct

*The list of examples stated at S. 18(a) to (d) is not exhaustive. It illustrates the type of conduct that will breach the Chapter II Prohibition. The recurring theme is exploitation which is achievable because the dominant undertaking can act independently and unchecked.*

### Section 18 (2) (a) Imposing unfair purchase or selling prices or other trading conditions

*Essentially a dominant company may abuse its position in the market by setting unfair and exploitative prices or conditions without fear of effective competition. The main purpose of such action is to increase profit at the expense of other competitors and the consumer.*

*In terms of 'unfair pricing' the authorities look for prices that are excessive because they bear no reasonable relation to the economic value of the product. Inevitably, the authorities subject the particular price to an economic analysis.*

*A dominant undertaking may also adopt the practise of 'predatory pricing' whereby it reduces its prices to a level where competitors cannot compete and are subsequently driven out of the market. As a result the undertaking will increase its market share and dominance.*

### Section 18 (2) (b) Limiting production, markets or technical development

*This example refers to the situation where a dominant undertaking limits the supply side of the market and controls future price levels. The purpose of such conduct is to protect profit and to preserve the undertaking's position of strength.*

### Section 18 (2) (c) Applying dissimilar conditions to equivalent transactions

*By applying dissimilar conditions the undertaking discriminates as to how it deals with customers in order to gain or protect its market. For example, such conduct may involve the undertaking offering discounts and rebates to one customer but not to another depending on where it needs to compete.*

**Section 18 (2) (d) Making the conclusion of contracts subject to acceptance by the other parties of supplementary obligations**

*An example of such conduct would occur when a dominant retailer demands a condition from a supplier that it does not supply competing retailers. Alternatively, a dominant supplier or manufacturer may demand a condition that a retailer does not stock similar products supplied by competing suppliers.*

(3) In this section-

"dominant position" means a dominant position within the United Kingdom; and

"the United Kingdom" means the United Kingdom or any part of it.

(4) The prohibition imposed by subsection (1) is referred to in this Act as "the Chapter II prohibition".

**Excluded cases**

**19.**– (1) The Chapter II prohibition does not apply in any of the cases in which it is excluded by or as a result of-

(a) Schedule 1 (mergers and concentrations); or
(b) Schedule 3 (general exclusions).

**Section 19 (1)**
*Cases excluded from the Chapter II Prohibition are contained within Schedule 1 which relates to mergers and concentrations and Schedule 3 covering general exclusions.*

(2) The Secretary of State may at any time by order amend Schedule 1, with respect to the Chapter II prohibition, by-

(a) providing for one or more additional exclusions; or
(b) amending or removing any provision (whether or not it has been added by an order under this subsection).

(3) The Secretary of State may at any time by order amend paragraph 8 of Schedule 3 with respect to the Chapter II prohibition.

(4) Schedule 3 also gives the Secretary of State power to provide that the Chapter II prohibition is not to apply in certain circumstances.

**Section 19 (2)-(4)**
*These sub-sections stipulate the powers of amendment by the Secretary of State in relation to the Schedules 1 and 3. He may add to the exclusions and may amend or remove any of the provisions.*

**Notification**

20.– (1) Sections 21 and 22 provide for conduct of a person which that person thinks may infringe the Chapter II prohibition to be considered by the Director on the application of that person.

(2) Schedule 6 provides for the procedure to be followed-

    (a) by any person making an application, and
    (b) by the Director, in considering an application.

**Section 20**
*(1)   This section introduces the 'notification procedure'. If an undertaking is concerned that it's conduct may infringe the Chapter II prohibition it may request consideration by the Director.*

*(2)   The application procedure is set out at Schedule 6.*

21.– (1) A person who applies for conduct to be considered under this section must-

    (a) notify the Director of it; and
    (b) apply to him for guidance.

(2) On an application under this section, the Director may give the applicant guidance as to whether or not, in his view, the conduct is likely to infringe the Chapter II prohibition.

**Section 21**
*The first option for the concerned undertaking is an application to the Director for guidance as to whether or not its conduct is likely to infringe the Chapter II prohibition. For the effect of guidance see section 23.*

22.– (1) A person who applies for conduct to be considered under this section must-

    (a) notify the Director of it; and

(b) apply to him for a decision.

(2) On an application under this section, the Director may make a decision as to-

(a) whether the Chapter II prohibition has been infringed; and

(b) if it has not been infringed, whether that is because of the effect of an exclusion.

---

**Section 22**
*The second option for the concerned undertaking is application to the Director for a decision as to whether or not its conduct has infringed the Chapter II prohibition. For the effect of a decision see section 24.*

---

**23.**– (1) This section applies to conduct if the Director has determined an application under section 21 by giving guidance that the conduct is unlikely to infringe the Chapter II prohibition.

(2) The Director is to take no further action under this Part with respect to the conduct to which this section applies, unless-

(a) he has reasonable grounds for believing that there has been a material change of circumstance since he gave his guidance;

(b) he has a reasonable suspicion that the information on which he based his guidance was incomplete, false or misleading in a material particular; or

(c) a complaint about the conduct has been made to him.

---

**Section 23**
*Once the Director has given guidance to an undertaking he is then limited in terms of taking further action in the matter. Look directly at the text at section 23(2)(a)-(c) for the grounds as to when he can re-open the file.*

---

(3) No penalty may be imposed under this Part in respect of any infringement of the Chapter II prohibition by conduct to which this section applies.

---

**Section 23 (3)**
*Providing notification of conduct has been given and guidance sought by the undertaking, no penalty can be imposed by the Director. However, this immunity is subject to the conditions set out in sub-sections (4) and (5) below.*

---

(4) But the Director may remove the immunity given by subsection (3) if-

    (a) he takes action under this Part with respect to the conduct in one of the circumstances mentioned in subsection (2);

    (b) he considers that it is likely that the conduct will infringe the prohibition; and

    (c) he gives notice in writing to the undertaking on whose application the guidance was given that he is removing the immunity as from the date specified in his notice.

> **Section 23 (4)**
> *The immunity from penalty may be removed under the grounds stated at (a) to (c) listed above.*

(5) If the Director has a reasonable suspicion that information-

    (a) on which he based his guidance, and

    (b) which was provided to him by an undertaking engaging in the conduct,

was incomplete, false or misleading in a material particular, the date specified in a notice under subsection (4)(c) may be earlier than the date on which the notice is given.

> **Section 23 (5)**
> *The Director may lift the immunity to a date before the notification if information from the undertaking had been incomplete, false or misleading. In effect, the immunity from penalty will lift entirely.*

**24.-** (1) This section applies to conduct if the Director has determined an application under section 22 by making a decision that the conduct has not infringed the Chapter II prohibition.

> **Section 24**
> *This section focuses on the effect of a decision by the Director. It is similar to section 23 in its wording but differs in that third party complaints will already have been considered and therefore, will not generate further action by the Director as would be the case under S. 23(2)(c).*

*The principal difference between a decision and guidance is the involvement of third parties. Essentially, third parties are invited to make representations. Invitation to the third parties may be made by publication of a general notice that will be published in the trade and national press or by specific invitation.*

*The views expressed by the third parties will be considered in addition to the analysis of the economic effects on the market and all other individual circumstances.*

(2) The Director is to take no further action under this Part with respect to the conduct unless-

    (a) he has reasonable grounds for believing that there has been a material change of circumstance since he gave his decision; or

    (b) he has a reasonable suspicion that the information on which he based his decision was incomplete, false or misleading in a material particular.

**Section 24 (2)**
*Once a decision has been made the Director is limited as to when he can take further action. Grounds for further action are stated at sub-sections (2)(a) and (b) and sub-section (5).*

(3) No penalty may be imposed under this Part in respect of any infringement of the Chapter II prohibition by conduct to which this section applies.

(4) But the Director may remove the immunity given by subsection (3) if-

    (a) he takes action under this Part with respect to the conduct in one of the circumstances mentioned in subsection (2);

    (b) he considers that it is likely that the conduct will infringe the prohibition; and

    (c) he gives notice in writing to the undertaking on whose application the decision was made that he is removing the immunity as from the date specified in his notice.

(5) If the Director has a reasonable suspicion that information-

    (a) on which he based his decision, and

    (b) which was provided to him by an undertaking engaging in the conduct,

was incomplete, false or misleading in a material particular, the date specified in a notice under subsection (4)(c) may be earlier than the date on which the notice is given.

**Section 24 (5)**
*The Director may lift the immunity to a date before the notification date if information supplied by the undertaking was incomplete, false or misleading.*

CHAPTER III

INVESTIGATION AND ENFORCEMENT

**Investigations**

25. The Director may conduct an investigation if there are reasonable grounds for suspecting-

    (a) that the Chapter I prohibition has been infringed; or
    (b) that the Chapter II prohibition has been infringed.

**Section 25**
*Investigations into alleged breaches of the Chapter I and Chapter II Prohibitions will be conducted by the Director General of Fair Trading. In order to conduct such an investigation the Director or his officers may only act if there are 'reasonable grounds for suspecting' that there has been an infringement.*

26.– (1) For the purposes of an investigation under section 25, the Director may require any person to produce to him a specified document, or to provide him with specified information, which he considers relates to any matter relevant to the investigation.

(2) The power conferred by subsection (1) is to be exercised by a notice in writing.

(3) A notice under subsection (2) must indicate-

    (a) the subject matter and purpose of the investigation; and
    (b) the nature of the offences created by sections 42 to 44.

(4) In subsection (1) "specified" means-

    (a) specified, or described, in the notice; or
    (b) falling within a category which is specified, or described, in the notice.

(5) The Director may also specify in the notice-

    (a) the time and place at which any document is to be produced or any information is to be provided;
    (b) the manner and form in which it is to be produced or provided.

(6) The power under this section to require a person to produce a document includes power-

    (a) if the document is produced-

        (i)  to take copies of it or extracts from it;

        (ii) to require him, or any person who is a present or past officer of his, or is or was at any time employed by him, to provide an explanation of the document;

    (b) if the document is not produced, to require him to state, to the best of his knowledge and belief, where it is.

**Section 26**
*This section sets out the Director's powers in relation to an investigation and specifically in relation to seeking relevant documents. He can require;*

–    *the production of specified documents or information;*

–    *copies of the documents or extracts from it;*

–    *explanations in relation to the documents; and*

–    *information concerning documents that have not been produced.*

27.– (1) Any officer of the Director who is authorised in writing by the Director to do so ("an investigating officer") may enter any premises in connection with an investigation under section 25.

**Section 27 (1)**
*An authorised investigating officer can enter 'any' premises relating to an investigation without a warrant subject to S. 27 (2) below.*

(2) No investigating officer is to enter any premises in the exercise of his powers under this section unless he has given to the occupier of the premises a written notice which-

    (a) gives at least two working days' notice of the intended entry;

    (b) indicates the subject matter and purpose of the investigation; and

    (c) indicates the nature of the offences created by sections 42 to 44.

> **Section 27 (2)**
> *Subject to sub-section (3) written notice must be given containing the following information;*
>
> – *two working days' notice of the intended entry;*
>
> – *the subject matter and purpose of the investigation; and*
>
> – *an indication as to the nature of the offences.*

(3) Subsection (2) does not apply-

   (a) if the Director has a reasonable suspicion that the premises are, or have been, occupied by-
      (i) a party to an agreement which he is investigating under section 25(a); or
      (ii) an undertaking the conduct of which he is investigating under section 25(b); or

   (b) if the investigating officer has taken all such steps as are reasonably practicable to give notice but has not been able to do so.

> **Section 27 (3)**
> *This sub-section enables the Director to enter without notice if he has reasonable suspicion that the premises are or have been occupied by a party whose agreement or conduct is subject to an investigation. Additionally, he may enter if he has taken all steps as are reasonably practicable to give notice but has not been able to do so.*

(4) In a case falling within subsection (3), the power of entry conferred by subsection (1) is to be exercised by the investigating officer on production of-

   (a) evidence of his authorisation; and
   (b) a document containing the information referred to in subsection (2)(b) and (c).

> **Section 27 (4)**
> *The investigating officer must produce authorisation, an indication as to the subject matter and purpose of the investigation and an indication as to the nature of the offences at the point of entry.*

(5) An investigating officer entering any premises under this section may-

   (a) take with him such equipment as appears to him to be necessary;

(b) require any person on the premises-
   (i) to produce any document which he considers relates to any matter relevant to the investigation; and
   (ii) if the document is produced, to provide an explanation of it;
(c) require any person to state, to the best of his knowledge and belief, where any such document is to be found;
(d) take copies of, or extracts from, any document which is produced;
(e) require any information which is held in a computer and is accessible from the premises and which the investigating officer considers relates to any matter relevant to the investigation, to be produced in a form-
   (i) in which it can be taken away, and
   (ii) in which it is visible and legible.

**Section 27 (5) (a) to (e)**
*An investigating officer may require;*

- *the production of relevant documents;*

- *copies or extracts of documents;*

- *explanations as to the whereabouts of certain documents;*

- *explanations as to the documents; and*

- *information held on computer.*

28.– (1) On an application made by the Director to the court in accordance with rules of court, a judge may issue a warrant if he is satisfied that-

(a) there are reasonable grounds for suspecting that there are on any premises documents-
   (i) the production of which has been required under section 26 or 27; and
   (ii) which have not been produced as required;
(b) there are reasonable grounds for suspecting that-
   (i) there are on any premises documents which the Director has power under section 26 to require to be produced; and
   (ii) if the documents were required to be produced, they would not be produced but would be concealed, removed, tampered with or destroyed; or
(c) an investigating officer has attempted to enter premises in the exercise of his powers under section 27 but has been unable to do so and that there are reasonable grounds for suspecting that there are on the premises documents the production of which could have been required under that section.

**Section 28 (1)**

*This section allows the Director to apply to the High Court for a warrant that will enable entry and search of premises without notice and to use such force as is reasonably necessary. The judge must be satisfied that there are reasonable grounds for suspecting that the premises contain documents which;*

— *have been required under s.26 or s.27 but not produced ;*

— *could be produced under s.26 but if the documents were required they would be concealed, removed, tampered with or destroyed; or*

— *an officer has attempted to enter under his section 27 powers but has not been able to do so.*

(2) A warrant under this section shall authorise a named officer of the Director, and any other of his officers whom he has authorised in writing to accompany the named officer-

(a) to enter the premises specified in the warrant, using such force as is reasonably necessary for the purpose;

(b) to search the premises and take copies of, or extracts from, any document appearing to be of a kind in respect of which the application under subsection (1) was granted ("the relevant kind");

(c) to take possession of any documents appearing to be of the relevant kind if-

(i) such action appears to be necessary for preserving the documents or preventing interference with them; or

(ii) it is not reasonably practicable to take copies of the documents on the premises;

(d) to take any other steps which appear to be necessary for the purpose mentioned in paragraph (c)(i);

(e) to require any person to provide an explanation of any document appearing to be of the relevant kind or to state, to the best of his knowledge and belief, where it may be found;

(f) to require any information which is held in a computer and is accessible from the premises and which the named officer considers relates to any matter relevant to the investigation, to be produced in a form-

(i) in which it can be taken away, and

(ii) in which it is visible and legible.

**Section 28 (2) (a) to (f)**

**Information contained in the warrant (please read in conjunction with S.29)**

– *the names of the officers must be specified in writing*

– *the premises must be specified*

– *the authority to enter using such force as is reasonably necessary*

– *the authority to search the premises and take any relevant document or copies or extracts from*

– *the authority to take possession of relevant documents to preserve or prevent interference with them*

– *the authority to take possession of relevant documents where it is not reasonably practicable to copy them*

– *the authority to take 'any other steps' which appear necessary in order to take possession of documents when it appears necessary to preserve them or to prevent interference with them*

– *the authority to require any person to provide an explanation as to a relevant document*

– *the authority to require any person to state where a relevant document may be found*

– *the authority to require any relevant information held in a computer to be produced in a form which is visible and legible and which enables the officers to take it away*

(3) If, in the case of a warrant under subsection (1)(b), the judge is satisfied that it is reasonable to suspect that there are also on the premises other documents relating to the investigation concerned, the warrant shall also authorise action mentioned in subsection (2) to be taken in relation to any such document.

(4) Any person entering premises by virtue of a warrant under this section may take with him such equipment as appears to him to be necessary.

(5) On leaving any premises which he has entered by virtue of a warrant under this section, the named officer must, if the premises are unoccupied or the occupier is temporarily absent, leave them as effectively secured as he found them.

(6) A warrant under this section continues in force until the end of the period of one month beginning with the day on which it is issued.

(7) Any document of which possession is taken under subsection (2)(c) may be retained for a period of three months.

**29.**– (1) A warrant issued under section 28 must indicate-

(a) the subject matter and purpose of the investigation;

(b) the nature of the offences created by sections 42 to 44.

---

**Section 29 (1)**

*This section supplements S.28 concerning the information contained in the warrant.*

*The warrant must also contain;*

– *the subject matter and purpose of the investigation*

– *the nature of the offences at sections 42 to 44*

---

(2) The powers conferred by section 28 are to be exercised on production of a warrant issued under that section.

(3) If there is no one at the premises when the named officer proposes to execute such a warrant he must, before executing it-

(a) take such steps as are reasonable in all the circumstances to inform the occupier of the intended entry; and

(b) if the occupier is informed, afford him or his legal or other representative a reasonable opportunity to be present when the warrant is executed.

---

**Section 29 (3) (a) and (b)**

*This sub-section guards against arbitrary action by the investigating officers. The officer who executes the warrant must 'take such steps as are reasonable in all the circumstances to inform the occupier of the intended entry.' If the occupier is informed the officer must give him, his lawyer or other representative 'reasonable opportunity' to be present when the warrant is executed.*

---

(4) If the named officer is unable to inform the occupier of the intended entry he must, when executing the warrant, leave a copy of it in a prominent place on the premises.

(5) In this section-

"named officer" means the officer named in the warrant; and

"occupier", in relation to any premises, means a person whom the named officer reasonably believes is the occupier of those premises.

**30.**– (1) A person shall not be required, under any provision of this Part, to produce or disclose a privileged communication.

(2) "Privileged communication" means a communication-

(a) between a professional legal adviser and his client, or
(b) made in connection with, or in contemplation of, legal proceedings and for the purposes of those proceedings,

which in proceedings in the High Court would be protected from disclosure on grounds of legal professional privilege.

(3) In the application of this section to Scotland-

(a) references to the High Court are to be read as references to the Court of Session; and
(b) the reference to legal professional privilege is to be read as a reference to confidentiality of communications.

**Section 30**
*Communications between undertakings and professional legal advisers are privileged and are excluded from the category of specified documents.*

**31.**– (1) Subsection (2) applies if, as the result of an investigation conducted under section 25, the Director proposes to make-

(a) a decision that the Chapter I prohibition has been infringed, or
(b) a decision that the Chapter II prohibition has been infringed.

(2) Before making the decision, the Director must-

(a) give written notice to the person (or persons) likely to be affected by the proposed decision; and
(b) give that person (or those persons) an opportunity to make representations.

**Section 31**
*Following an investigation, the Director may make a decision in relation to an alleged infringement. Before doing so he must give notice to the affected persons and allow representations.*

## Enforcement

**32.**– (1) If the Director has made a decision that an agreement infringes the Chapter I prohibition, he may give to such person or persons as he considers appropriate such directions as he considers appropriate to bring the infringement to an end.

(2) Subsection (1) applies whether the Director's decision is made on his own initiative or on an application made to him under this Part.

(3) A direction under this section may, in particular, include provision-

(a) requiring the parties to the agreement to modify the agreement; or
(b) requiring them to terminate the agreement.

(4) A direction under this section must be given in writing.

> **Section 32**
> *Following a decision made by the Director in relation to an infringement of the Chapter I Prohibition, he may make certain written directions requiring the parties to make modifications or terminate the agreement.*

33.– (1) If the Director has made a decision that conduct infringes the Chapter II prohibition, he may give to such person or persons as he considers appropriate such directions as he considers appropriate to bring the infringement to an end.

(2) Subsection (1) applies whether the Director's decision is made on his own initiative or on an application made to him under this Part.

(3) A direction under this section may, in particular, include provision-

(a) requiring the person concerned to modify the conduct in question; or
(b) requiring him to cease that conduct.

(4) A direction under this section must be given in writing.

> **Section 33**
> *Similarly the Director can issue written directions that require modification or termination of offending conduct under the Chapter II Prohibition.*

34.– (1) If a person fails, without reasonable excuse, to comply with a direction under section 32 or 33, the Director may apply to the court for an order-

(a) requiring the defaulter to make good his default within a time specified in the order; or
(b) if the direction related to anything to be done in the management or administration of an undertaking, requiring the undertaking or any of its officers to do it.

(2) An order of the court under subsection (1) may provide for all of the costs of, or incidental to, the application for the order to be borne by-

(a) the person in default; or

(b) any officer of an undertaking who is responsible for the default.

(3) In the application of subsection (2) to Scotland, the reference to "costs" is to be read as a reference to "expenses".

**Section 34**
*The Director may apply for a court order to enforce directions under S.32 and S.33 if the undertakings fail to comply without a reasonable excuse.*

35.– (1) This section applies if the Director-

(a) has a reasonable suspicion that the Chapter I prohibition has been infringed, or

(b) has a reasonable suspicion that the Chapter II prohibition has been infringed,

but has not completed his investigation into the matter.

(2) If the Director considers that it is necessary for him to act under this section as a matter of urgency for the purpose-

(a) of preventing serious, irreparable damage to a particular person or category of person, or

(b) of protecting the public interest,

he may give such directions as he considers appropriate for that purpose.

(3) Before giving a direction under this section, the Director must-

(a) give written notice to the person (or persons) to whom he proposes to give the direction; and

(b) give that person (or each of them) an opportunity to make representations.

(4) A notice under subsection (3) must indicate the nature of the direction which the Director is proposing to give and his reasons for wishing to give it.

(5) A direction given under this section has effect while subsection (1) applies, but may be replaced if the circumstances permit by a direction under section 32 or (as appropriate) section 33.

(6) In the case of a suspected infringement of the Chapter I prohibition, sections 32(3) and 34 also apply to directions given under this section.

(7) In the case of a suspected infringement of the Chapter II prohibition, sections 33(3) and 34 also apply to directions given under this section.

**Section 35**

*This section enables the Director to make directions whilst an investigation takes place. If he has 'reasonable suspicion' that a Chapter I or Chapter II infringement has occurred he may make such directions 'as he considers appropriate' for the purpose of;*

i. *preventing serious, irreparable damage to a particular person or category of persons; or*

ii. *protecting the public interest.*

*However, before he issues such directions the Director must give notice in writing to the persons concerned and the opportunity to make representations.*

*The notice must state the nature and the reasons for the proposed direction.*

*The direction can apply for as long as the infringement is suspected and the investigation remains incomplete.*

*On completion of the investigation the interim directions may be replaced by final directions.*

36.– (1) On making a decision that an agreement has infringed the Chapter I prohibition, the Director may require an undertaking which is a party to the agreement to pay him a penalty in respect of the infringement.

(2) On making a decision that conduct has infringed the Chapter II prohibition, the Director may require the undertaking concerned to pay him a penalty in respect of the infringement.

**Section 36 (1) and (2)**

*These sub-sections provide for the imposition of penalties by the Director in relation to both the Chapter I and Chapter II Prohibitions. The penalties take the form of a civil debt.*

(3) The Director may impose a penalty on an undertaking under subsection (1) or (2) only if he is satisfied that the infringement has been committed intentionally or negligently by the undertaking.

**Section 36 (3)**

*Penalties will be imposed on both intentional and negligent infringements.*

(4) Subsection (1) is subject to section 39 and does not apply if the Director is satisfied that the undertaking acted on the reasonable assumption that that section gave it immunity in respect of the agreement.

> **Section 36 (4)**
> *In relation to the Chapter I Prohibition, an undertaking will be afforded a defence if the Director is satisfied that the persons concerned acted on the reasonable assumption that the agreement was immune under section 39.*

(5) Subsection (2) is subject to section 40 and does not apply if the Director is satisfied that the undertaking acted on the reasonable assumption that that section gave it immunity in respect of the conduct.

> **Section 36 (5)**
> *In relation to the Chapter II Prohibition, an undertaking will be afforded a defence if the Director is satisfied that the persons concerned acted on the reasonable assumption that the conduct was immune under section 40.*

(6) Notice of a penalty under this section must-

    (a) be in writing; and
    (b) specify the date before which the penalty is required to be paid.

> **Section 36 (6)**
> *Notice relating to penalties.*

(7) The date specified must not be earlier than the end of the period within which an appeal against the notice may be brought under section 46.

(8) No penalty fixed by the Director under this section may exceed 10% of the turnover of the undertaking (determined in accordance with such provisions as may be specified in an order made by the Secretary of State).

> **Section 36 (8)**
> *The Director may impose a penalty not exceeding 10% of the undertaking's turnover.*

(9) Any sums received by the Director under this section are to be paid into the Consolidated Fund.

**37.**– (1) If the specified date in a penalty notice has passed and-

    (a) the period during which an appeal against the imposition, or amount, of the penalty may be made has expired without an appeal having been made, or

    (b) such an appeal has been made and determined,

the Director may recover from the undertaking, as a civil debt due to him, any amount payable under the penalty notice which remains outstanding.

(2) In this section-

    "penalty notice" means a notice given under section 36; and

    "specified date" means the date specified in the penalty notice.

**Section 37**
*Unless the case is subject to appeal proceedings, the Director may recover the penalty debt not paid by the date specified in the penalty notice.*

**38.**– (1) The Director must prepare and publish guidance as to the appropriate amount of any penalty under this Part.

(2) The Director may at any time alter the guidance.

(3) If the guidance is altered, the Director must publish it as altered.

(4) No guidance is to be published under this section without the approval of the Secretary of State.

(5) The Director may, after consulting the Secretary of State, choose how he publishes his guidance.

(6) If the Director is preparing or altering guidance under this section he must consult such persons as he considers appropriate.

(7) If the proposed guidance or alteration relates to a matter in respect of which a regulator exercises concurrent jurisdiction, those consulted must include that regulator.

(8) When setting the amount of a penalty under this Part, the Director must have regard to the guidance for the time being in force under this section.

(9) If a penalty or a fine has been imposed by the Commission, or by a court or other body in another Member State, in respect of an agreement or conduct, the Director, an appeal tribunal or the appropriate court must take that penalty or fine into account when setting the amount of a penalty under this Part in relation to that agreement or conduct.

(10) In subsection (9) "the appropriate court" means-

    (a) in relation to England and Wales, the Court of Appeal;

    (b) in relation to Scotland, the Court of Session;

    (c) in relation to Northern Ireland, the Court of Appeal in Northern Ireland;

    (d) the House of Lords.

**Section 38**

*This section refers to the level of penalties. The Director is required to publish guidance in relation to appropriate amounts.*

*When a fine is being considered the Director or the appropriate court must have regard to the guidance published by the Director.*

**39.–** (1) In this section "small agreement" means an agreement-

    (a) which falls within a category prescribed for the purposes of this section; but

    (b) is not a price fixing agreement.

**Section 39**

*This section provides an immunity in relation to agreements that are considered to have a minimal effect on competition in the market. However, the immunity will not apply to 'price fixing agreements.' (see definition at section 39(9).*

*The Chapter I Prohibition only deals with agreements that have an appreciable or significant effect on competition.*

(2) The criteria by reference to which a category of agreement is prescribed may, in particular, include-

    (a) the combined turnover of the parties to the agreement (determined in accordance with prescribed provisions);

    (b) the share of the market affected by the agreement (determined in that way).

**Section 39 (2)**

*This section refers to the important criteria relating to 'small agreements'. Point (a) refers to the combined turnover of the parties involved. Point (b) specifically refers to 'the share of the market affected by the agreement'.*

(3) A party to a small agreement is immune from the effect of section 36(1); but the Director may withdraw that immunity under subsection (4).

(4) If the Director has investigated a small agreement, he may make a decision withdrawing the immunity given by subsection (3) if, as a result of his investigation, he considers that the agreement is likely to infringe the Chapter I prohibition.

### Section 39 (4)
*The Director can withdraw the immunity.*

(5) The Director must give each of the parties in respect of which immunity is withdrawn written notice of his decision to withdraw the immunity.

(6) A decision under subsection (4) takes effect on such date ("the withdrawal date") as may be specified in the decision.

(7) The withdrawal date must be a date after the date on which the decision is made.

(8) In determining the withdrawal date, the Director must have regard to the amount of time which the parties are likely to require in order to secure that there is no further infringement of the Chapter I prohibition with respect to the agreement.

(9) In subsection (1) "price fixing agreement" means an agreement which has as its object or effect, or one of its objects or effects, restricting the freedom of a party to the agreement to determine the price to be charged (otherwise than as between that party and another party to the agreement) for the product, service or other matter to which the agreement relates.

40.– (1) In this section "conduct of minor significance" means conduct which falls within a category prescribed for the purposes of this section.

(2) The criteria by reference to which a category is prescribed may, in particular, include-

  (a) the turnover of the person whose conduct it is (determined in accordance with prescribed provisions);
  (b) the share of the market affected by the conduct (determined in that way).

(3) A person is immune from the effect of section 36(2) if his conduct is conduct of minor significance; but the Director may withdraw that immunity under subsection (4).

**Section 40**
*This section refers to conduct which is of 'minor significance' and may be immune from penalty. S.40 (2) (a) and (b) refers to the criteria that the Director will use in determining whether the conduct is of a minor significance;*

i.    *the turnover of the undertaking; and*

ii.   *the share of the market affected by the conduct.*

(4) If the Director has investigated conduct of minor significance, he may make a decision withdrawing the immunity given by subsection (3) if, as a result of his investigation, he considers that the conduct is likely to infringe the Chapter II prohibition.

**Secetion 40 (4)**
*The Director has the power to withdraw the immunity.*

(5) The Director must give the person, or persons, whose immunity has been withdrawn written notice of his decision to withdraw the immunity.

(6) A decision under subsection (4) takes effect on such date ("the withdrawal date") as may be specified in the decision.

(7) The withdrawal date must be a date after the date on which the decision is made.

(8) In determining the withdrawal date, the Director must have regard to the amount of time which the person or persons affected are likely to require in order to secure that there is no further infringement of the Chapter II prohibition.

**41.–** (1) This section applies if a party to an agreement which may infringe the Chapter I prohibition has notified the agreement to the Commission for a decision as to whether an exemption will be granted under Article 85 with respect to the agreement.

(2) A penalty may not be required to be paid under this Part in respect of any infringement of the Chapter I prohibition after notification but before the Commission determines the matter.

(3) If the Commission withdraws the benefit of provisional immunity from penalties with respect to the agreement, subsection (2) ceases to apply as from the date on which that benefit is withdrawn.

(4) The fact that an agreement has been notified to the Commission does not prevent the Director from investigating it under this Part.

(5) In this section "provisional immunity from penalties" has such meaning as may be prescribed.

> ### Section 41
> *This section provides an interim immunity to agreements that may infringe the Chapter I Prohibition but the concerned undertaking has notified the European Commission of the agreement under EC competition law.*
>
> *However, the Commission may withdraw the 'provisional immunity.'*

### Offences

42.– (1) A person is guilty of an offence if he fails to comply with a requirement imposed on him under section 26, 27 or 28.

> ### Section 42
> *This section creates criminal offences in relation to non-compliance with investigations. Specifically, an individual is required to comply with requirements under sections 26, 27 or 28.*

(2) If a person is charged with an offence under subsection (1) in respect of a requirement to produce a document, it is a defence for him to prove-

    (a) that the document was not in his possession or under his control; and
    (b) that it was not reasonably practicable for him to comply with the requirement.

(3) If a person is charged with an offence under subsection (1) in respect of a requirement-

    (a) to provide information,
    (b) to provide an explanation of a document, or
    (c) to state where a document is to be found,

it is a defence for him to prove that he had a reasonable excuse for failing to comply with the requirement.

(4) Failure to comply with a requirement imposed under section 26 or 27 is not an offence if the person imposing the requirement has failed to act in accordance with that section.

**Section 42 (2)-(4)**
*These sub-sections stipulate defences to the offences.*

(5) A person is guilty of an offence if he intentionally obstructs an officer acting in the exercise of his powers under section 27.

(6) A person guilty of an offence under subsection (1) or (5) is liable-

(a) on summary conviction, to a fine not exceeding the statutory maximum;
(b) on conviction on indictment, to a fine.

(7) A person who intentionally obstructs an officer in the exercise of his powers under a warrant issued under section 28 is guilty of an offence and liable-

(a) on summary conviction, to a fine not exceeding the statutory maximum;
(b) on conviction on indictment, to imprisonment for a term not exceeding two years or to a fine or to both.

**Section 42 (6) and (7)**
*These sub-sections state the penalties for non-compliance with the investigation.*

**43.–** (1) A person is guilty of an offence if, having been required to produce a document under section 26, 27 or 28-

(a) he intentionally or recklessly destroys or otherwise disposes of it, falsifies it or conceals it, or
(b) he causes or permits its destruction, disposal, falsification or concealment.

**Section 43**
*This section creates further criminal offences. See text.*

(2) A person guilty of an offence under subsection (1) is liable-

(a) on summary conviction, to a fine not exceeding the statutory maximum;
(b) on conviction on indictment, to imprisonment for a term not exceeding two years or to a fine or to both.

> **Section 43 (2)**
> *This sub-section states the penalties for such offences.*

**44.**– (1) If information is provided by a person to the Director in connection with any function of the Director under this Part, that person is guilty of an offence if-

    (a) the information is false or misleading in a material particular, and
    (b) he knows that it is or is reckless as to whether it is.

(2) A person who-

    (a) provides any information to another person, knowing the information to be false or misleading in a material particular, or
    (b) recklessly provides any information to another person which is false or misleading in a material particular,

knowing that the information is to be used for the purpose of providing information to the Director in connection with any of his functions under this Part, is guilty of an offence.

(3) A person guilty of an offence under this section is liable-

    (a) on summary conviction, to a fine not exceeding the statutory maximum;
    (b) on conviction on indictment, to imprisonment for a term not exceeding two years or to a fine or to both.

> **Section 44**
> *This section creates an offence of knowingly or recklessly providing false or misleading information. S. 44(3) states the penalty for this offence.*

### CHAPTER IV

### THE COMPETITION COMMISSION AND APPEALS

**The Commission**

**45.**– (1) There is to be a body corporate known as the Competition Commission.

(2) The Commission is to have such functions as are conferred on it by or as a result of this Act.

(3) The Monopolies and Mergers Commission is dissolved and its functions are transferred to the Competition Commission.

(4) In any enactment, instrument or other document, any reference to the Monopolies and Mergers Commission which has continuing effect is to be read as a reference to the Competition Commission.

(5) The Secretary of State may by order make such consequential, supplemental and incidental provision as he considers appropriate in connection with-

(a) the dissolution of the Monopolies and Mergers Commission; and
(b) the transfer of functions effected by subsection (3).

(6) An order made under subsection (5) may, in particular, include provision-

(a) for the transfer of property, rights, obligations and liabilities and the continuation of proceedings, investigations and other matters; or
(b) amending any enactment which makes provision with respect to the Monopolies and Mergers Commission or any of its functions.

(7) Schedule 7 makes further provision about the Competition Commission.

**Section 45**
*This section creates a new body called the Competition Commission. The Monopolies and Mergers Commission is dissolved and it's functions transfer to the new Commission.*

*Schedule 7 provides further detailed provision.*

## Appeals

**46.**– (1) Any party to an agreement in respect of which the Director has made a decision may appeal to the Competition Commission against, or with respect to, the decision.

(2) Any person in respect of whose conduct the Director has made a decision may appeal to the Competition Commission against, or with respect to, the decision.

(3) In this section "decision" means a decision of the Director-

(a) as to whether the Chapter I prohibition has been infringed,
(b) as to whether the Chapter II prohibition has been infringed,
(c) as to whether to grant an individual exemption,
(d) in respect of an individual exemption-
   (i) as to whether to impose any condition or obligation under section 4(3)(a) or 5(1)(c),
   (ii) where such a condition or obligation has been imposed, as to the condition or obligation,
   (iii) as to the period fixed under section 4(3)(b), or
   (iv) as to the date fixed under section 4(5),

(e) as to-

   (i) whether to extend the period for which an individual exemption has effect, or

   (ii) the period of any such extension,

(f) cancelling an exemption,

(g) as to the imposition of any penalty under section 36 or as to the amount of any such penalty,

(h) withdrawing or varying any of the decisions in paragraphs (a) to (f) following an application under section 47(1),

and includes a direction given under section 32, 33 or 35 and such other decision as may be prescribed.

(4) Except in the case of an appeal against the imposition, or the amount, of a penalty, the making of an appeal under this section does not suspend the effect of the decision to which the appeal relates.

(5) Part I of Schedule 8 makes further provision about appeals.

## Section 46

*Appeals by parties to an agreement or whose conduct has been subject to a decision made by the Director and the regulators will be heard at the Competition Commission. Part I of Schedule 8 provides further detail on appeals.*

47.– (1) A person who does not fall within section 46(1) or (2) may apply to the Director asking him to withdraw or vary a decision ("the relevant decision") falling within paragraphs (a) to (f) of section 46(3) or such other decision as may be prescribed.

(2) The application must-

   (a) be made in writing, within such period as the Director may specify in rules under section 51; and

   (b) give the applicant's reasons for considering that the relevant decision should be withdrawn or (as the case may be) varied.

(3) If the Director decides-

   (a) that the applicant does not have a sufficient interest in the relevant decision,

   (b) that, in the case of an applicant claiming to represent persons who have such an interest, the applicant does not represent such persons, or

   (c) that the persons represented by the applicant do not have such an interest,

he must notify the applicant of his decision.

(4) If the Director, having considered the application, decides that it does not show sufficient reason why he should withdraw or vary the relevant decision, he must notify the applicant of his decision.

(5) Otherwise, the Director must deal with the application in accordance with such procedure as may be specified in rules under section 51.

(6) The applicant may appeal to the Competition Commission against a decision of the Director notified under subsection (3) or (4).

(7) The making of an application does not suspend the effect of the relevant decision.

**Section 47**
*This section provides 'third parties' with a sufficient interest in a particular decision with a right to apply to the Director to withdraw or vary it. This decision to withdraw or vary the original decision may also be appealed to the Competition Commission.*

**48.**– (1) Any appeal made to the Competition Commission under section 46 or 47 is to be determined by an appeal tribunal.

(2) The Secretary of State may, after consulting the President of the Competition Commission Appeal Tribunals and such other persons as he considers appropriate, make rules with respect to appeals and appeal tribunals.

(3) The rules may confer functions on the President.

(4) Part II of Schedule 8 makes further provision about rules made under this section but is not to be taken as restricting the Secretary of State's powers under this section.

**Section 48**
*This section creates the appeal tribunal within the Competition Commission.*

*Part II of Schedule 8 provides further detailed provision concerning the rules relating to appeals.*

**49.**– (1) An appeal lies-

(a) on a point of law arising from a decision of an appeal tribunal, or
(b) from any decision of an appeal tribunal as to the amount of a penalty.

(2) An appeal under this section may be made only-

    (a) to the appropriate court;

    (b) with leave; and

    (c) at the instance of a party or at the instance of a person who has a sufficient interest in the matter.

(3) Rules under section 48 may make provision for regulating or prescribing any matters incidental to or consequential upon an appeal under this section.

(4) In subsection (2)-

"the appropriate court" means-

    (a) in relation to proceedings before a tribunal in England and Wales, the Court of Appeal;

    (b) in relation to proceedings before a tribunal in Scotland, the Court of Session;

    (c) in relation to proceedings before a tribunal in Northern Ireland, the Court of Appeal in Northern Ireland;

"leave" means leave of the tribunal in question or of the appropriate court; and

"party", in relation to a decision, means a person who was a party to the proceedings in which the decision was made.

### Section 49
*Judgements made by the tribunal at the Competition Commission can be appealed to the Court of Appeal in England, Wales and Northern Ireland and the Court of Session in Scotland. However, such appeals will only relate to points of law and levels of penalty.*

CHAPTER V

MISCELLANEOUS

**Vertical agreements and land agreements**

**50.**- (1) The Secretary of State may by order provide for any provision of this Part to apply in relation to-

    (a) vertical agreements, or

    (b) land agreements,

with such modifications as may be prescribed.

(2) An order may, in particular, provide for exclusions or exemptions, or otherwise provide for prescribed provisions not to apply, in relation to-

(a) vertical agreements, or land agreements, in general; or
(b) vertical agreements, or land agreements, of any prescribed description.

(3) An order may empower the Director to give directions to the effect that in prescribed circumstances an exclusion, exemption or modification is not to apply (or is to apply in a particular way) in relation to an individual agreement.

(4) Subsections (2) and (3) are not to be read as limiting the powers conferred by section 71.

(5) In this section-

"land agreement" and "vertical agreement" have such meaning as may be prescribed; and

"prescribed" means prescribed by an order.

> **Section 50**
> *This section allows the Secretary of State the power to apply the provisions of Part I of the Act to 'vertical agreements' or 'land agreements'.*

## Director's rules, guidance and fees

**51.**– (1) The Director may make such rules about procedural and other matters in connection with the carrying into effect of the provisions of this Part as he considers appropriate.

(2) Schedule 9 makes further provision about rules made under this section but is not to be taken as restricting the Director's powers under this section.

(3) If the Director is preparing rules under this section he must consult such persons as he considers appropriate.

(4) If the proposed rules relate to a matter in respect of which a regulator exercises concurrent jurisdiction, those consulted must include that regulator.

(5) No rule made by the Director is to come into operation until it has been approved by an order made by the Secretary of State.

(6) The Secretary of State may approve any rule made by the Director-

(a) in the form in which it is submitted; or
(b) subject to such modifications as he considers appropriate.

(7) If the Secretary of State proposes to approve a rule subject to modifications he must inform the Director of the proposed modifications and take into account any comments made by the Director.

(8) Subsections (5) to (7) apply also to any alteration of the rules made by the Director.

(9) The Secretary of State may, after consulting the Director, by order vary or revoke any rules made under this section.

(10) If the Secretary of State considers that rules should be made under this section with respect to a particular matter he may direct the Director to exercise his powers under this section and make rules about that matter.

**Section 51**
*This section allows the Director the power to make procedural rules in relation to Part I of this Act. The section also introduces Schedule 9 on Director's rules.*

52.– (1) As soon as is reasonably practicable after the passing of this Act, the Director must prepare and publish general advice and information about-

(a) the application of the Chapter I prohibition and the Chapter II prohibition, and
(b) the enforcement of those prohibitions.

(2) The Director may at any time publish revised, or new, advice or information.

(3) Advice and information published under this section must be prepared with a view to-

(a) explaining provisions of this Part to persons who are likely to be affected by them; and
(b) indicating how the Director expects such provisions to operate.

(4) Advice (or information) published by virtue of subsection (3)(b) may include advice (or information) about the factors which the Director may take into account in considering whether, and if so how, to exercise a power conferred on him by Chapter I, II or III.

(5) Any advice or information published by the Director under this section is to be published in such form and in such manner as he considers appropriate.

(6) If the Director is preparing any advice or information under this section he must consult such persons as he considers appropriate.

(7) If the proposed advice or information relates to a matter in respect of which a regulator exercises concurrent jurisdiction, those consulted must include that regulator.

(8) In preparing any advice or information under this section about a matter in respect of which he may exercise functions under this Part, a regulator must consult-

(a) the Director;
(b) the other regulators; and
(c) such other persons as he considers appropriate.

**Section 52**
*This section imposes an obligation upon the Director to publish general advice and information relating to the application and enforcement of both Prohibitions.*

**53.**– (1) The Director may charge fees, of specified amounts, in connection with the exercise by him of specified functions under this Part.

(2) Rules may, in particular, provide-

   (a) for the amount of any fee to be calculated by reference to matters which may include-
      (i)  the turnover of any party to an agreement (determined in such manner as may be specified);
      (ii) the turnover of a person whose conduct the Director is to consider (determined in that way);
   (b) for different amounts to be specified in connection with different functions;
   (c) for the repayment by the Director of the whole or part of a fee in specified circumstances;
   (d) that an application or notice is not to be regarded as duly made or given unless the appropriate fee is paid.

(3) In this section-

   (a) "rules" means rules made by the Director under section 51; and
   (b) "specified" means specified in rules.

**Section 53**
*The Director will be entitled to charge fees relating to the exercise of specified functions set out in the rules under this part of the Act.*

**Regulators**

**54.**– (1) In this Part "regulator" means any person mentioned in paragraphs (a) to (g) of paragraph 1 of Schedule 10.

(2) Parts II and III of Schedule 10 provide for functions of the Director under this Part to be exercisable concurrently by regulators.

(3) Parts IV and V of Schedule 10 make minor and consequential amendments in connection with the regulators' competition functions.

(4) The Secretary of State may make regulations for the purpose of co-ordinating the performance of functions under this Part ("Part I functions") which are exercisable concurrently by two or more competent persons as a result of any provision made by Part II or III of Schedule 10.

(5) The regulations may, in particular, make provision-

    (a) as to the procedure to be followed by competent persons when determining who is to exercise Part I functions in a particular case;

    (b) as to the steps which must be taken before a competent person exercises, in a particular case, such Part I functions as may be prescribed;

    (c) as to the procedure for determining, in a particular case, questions arising as to which competent person is to exercise Part I functions in respect of the case;

    (d) for Part I functions in a particular case to be exercised jointly-

        (i) by the Director and one or more regulators, or

        (ii) by two or more regulators,

and as to the procedure to be followed in such cases;

    (e) as to the circumstances in which the exercise by a competent person of such Part I functions as may be prescribed is to preclude the exercise of such functions by another such person;

    (f) for cases in respect of which Part I functions are being, or have been, exercised by a competent person to be transferred to another such person;

    (g) for the person ("A") exercising Part I functions in a particular case-

        (i) to appoint another competent person ("B") to exercise Part I functions on A's behalf in relation to the case; or

        (ii) to appoint officers of B (with B's consent) to act as officers of A in relation to the case;

    (h) for notification as to who is exercising Part I functions in respect of a particular case.

(6) Provision made by virtue of subsection (5)(c) may provide for questions to be referred to and determined by the Secretary of State or by such other person as may be prescribed.

(7) "Competent person" means the Director or any of the regulators.

> **Section 54**
> *This section introduces Schedule 10 relating to Directors General in the regulated utility sectors who will exercise concurrent functions within their sectors.*

## Confidentiality and immunity from defamation

55.– (1) No information which-

(a) has been obtained under or as a result of any provision of this Part, and

(b) relates to the affairs of any individual or to any particular business of an undertaking,

is to be disclosed during the lifetime of that individual or while that business continues to be carried on, unless the condition mentioned in subsection (2) is satisfied.

> **Section 55**
> *This section prohibits the disclosure of information which has been obtained from individuals or from businesses during the lifetime of the person or whilst the business continues subject to sub-sections (2) and (3) below.*

(2) The condition is that consent to the disclosure has been obtained from-

(a) the person from whom the information was initially obtained under or as a result of any provision of this Part (if the identity of that person is known); and

(b) if different-

(i) the individual to whose affairs the information relates, or

(ii) the person for the time being carrying on the business to which the information relates.

> **Section 55 (2)**
> *The rule will not apply if the person or persons involved consent to the disclosure of the information.*

(3) Subsection (1) does not apply to a disclosure of information-

(a) made for the purpose of-

(i) facilitating the performance of any relevant functions of a designated person;

(ii) facilitating the performance of any functions of the Commission in respect of Community law about competition;

(iii) facilitating the performance by the Comptroller and Auditor General of any of his functions;

(iv) criminal proceedings in any part of the United Kingdom;

(b) made with a view to the institution of, or otherwise for the purposes of, civil proceedings brought under or in connection with this Part;

---

**Section 55 (3) (a)-(b)**

*Sub-sections (a) and (b) represent the exceptions to the general rule of confidentiality.*

*'Relevant functions' and 'designated person' are defined in Schedule 11.*

---

    (c) made in connection with the investigation of any criminal offence triable in the United Kingdom or in any part of the United Kingdom; or

    (d) which is required to meet a Community obligation.

(4) In subsection (3) "relevant functions" and "designated person" have the meaning given in Schedule 11.

(5) Subsection (1) also does not apply to a disclosure of information made for the purpose of facilitating the performance of specified functions of any specified person.

(6) In subsection (5) "specified" means specified in an order made by the Secretary of State.

(7) If information is disclosed to the public in circumstances in which the disclosure does not contravene subsection (1), that subsection does not prevent its further disclosure by any person.

(8) A person who contravenes this section is guilty of an offence and liable-

    (a) on summary conviction, to a fine not exceeding the statutory maximum; or

    (b) on conviction on indictment, to imprisonment for a term not exceeding two years or to a fine or to both.

---

**Section 55 (8)**

*This sub-section creates a criminal offence for unauthorised disclosure of information.*

---

**56.–** (1) This section applies if the Secretary of State or the Director is considering whether to disclose any information acquired by him under, or as a result of, any provision of this Part.

(2) He must have regard to the need for excluding, so far as is practicable, information the disclosure of which would in his opinion be contrary to the public interest.

(3) He must also have regard to-

    (a) the need for excluding, so far as is practicable-

    (i)  commercial information the disclosure of which would, or might, in his opinion, significantly harm the legitimate business interests of the undertaking to which it relates, or

    (ii)  information relating to the private affairs of an individual the disclosure of which would, or might, in his opinion, significantly harm his interests; and

  (b)  the extent to which the disclosure is necessary for the purposes for which the Secretary of State or the Director is proposing to make the disclosure.

---

**Section 56**

*If the Director or the Secretary of State consider disclosing information they must have regard to the extent to which disclosure is necessary and whether it will;*

–   *be contrary to the public interest;*

–   *significantly harm legitimate business interests of the undertaking; and/or*

–   *relate to private affairs of individuals concerned and disclosure would harm their interest.*

---

57.  For the purposes of the law relating to defamation, absolute privilege attaches to any advice, guidance, notice or direction given, or decision made, by the Director in the exercise of any of his functions under this Part.

---

**Section 57**

*This section places absolute privilege upon advice, notices and directions made by the Director in relation to the law of defamation.*

---

**Findings of fact by Director**

58.– (1)  Unless the court directs otherwise or the Director has decided to take further action in accordance with section 16(2) or 24(2), a Director's finding which is relevant to an issue arising in Part I proceedings is binding on the parties if-

  (a)  the time for bringing an appeal in respect of the finding has expired and the relevant party has not brought such an appeal; or

  (b)  the decision of an appeal tribunal on such an appeal has confirmed the finding.

(2)  In this section-

  "a Director's finding" means a finding of fact made by the Director in the course of-

  (a)  determining an application for a decision under section 14 or 22, or

  (b)  conducting an investigation under section 25;

"Part I proceedings" means proceedings-

(a) in respect of an alleged infringement of the Chapter I prohibition or of the Chapter II prohibition; but
(b) which are brought otherwise than by the Director;

"relevant party" means-

(a) in relation to the Chapter I prohibition, a party to the agreement which is alleged to have infringed the prohibition; and
(b) in relation to the Chapter II prohibition, the undertaking whose conduct is alleged to have infringed the prohibition.

(3) Rules of court may make provision in respect of assistance to be given by the Director to the court in Part I proceedings.

**Section 58**
*This section makes the Director's finding of facts in relation to an issue under this Part as binding on the parties unless a court directs otherwise.*

**Interpretation and governing principles**

**59.**– (1) In this Part-

"appeal tribunal" means an appeal tribunal established in accordance with the provisions of Part III of Schedule 7 for the purpose of hearing an appeal under section 46 or 47;

"Article 85" means Article 85 of the Treaty;

"Article 86" means Article 86 of the Treaty;

"block exemption" has the meaning given in section 6(4);

"block exemption order" has the meaning given in section 6(2);

"the Chapter I prohibition" has the meaning given in section 2(8);

"the Chapter II prohibition" has the meaning given in section 18(4);

"the Commission" (except in relation to the Competition Commission) means the European Commission;

"the Council" means the Council of the European Union;

"the court", except in sections 58 and 60 and the expression

"European Court", means-

(a) in England and Wales, the High Court;
(b) in Scotland, the Court of Session; and
(c) in Northern Ireland, the High Court;

"the Director" means the Director General of Fair Trading;

"document" includes information recorded in any form;

"the EEA Agreement" means the Agreement on the European Economic Area signed at Oporto on 2nd May 1992 as it has effect for the time being;

"the European Court" means the Court of Justice of the European Communities and includes the Court of First Instance;

"individual exemption" has the meaning given in section 4(2);

"information" includes estimates and forecasts;

"investigating officer" has the meaning given in section 27(1);

"Minister of the Crown" has the same meaning as in the Ministers of the Crown Act 1975;

"officer", in relation to a body corporate, includes a director, manager or secretary and, in relation to a partnership in Scotland, includes a partner;

"parallel exemption" has the meaning given in section 10(3);

"person", in addition to the meaning given by the Interpretation Act 1978, includes any undertaking;

"premises" does not include domestic premises unless-

(a) they are also used in connection with the affairs of an undertaking, or
(b) documents relating to the affairs of an undertaking are kept there,

but does include any vehicle;

"prescribed" means prescribed by regulations made by the Secretary of State;

"regulator" has the meaning given by section 54;

"section 11 exemption" has the meaning given in section 11(3); and

"the Treaty" means the treaty establishing the European Community.

(2) The fact that to a limited extent the Chapter I prohibition does not apply to an agreement, because of an exclusion provided by or under this Part or any other enactment, does not require those provisions of the agreement to which the exclusion relates to be disregarded when considering whether the agreement infringes the prohibition for other reasons.

(3) For the purposes of this Part, the power to require information, in relation to information recorded otherwise than in a legible form, includes power to require a copy of it in a legible form.

(4) Any power conferred on the Director by this Part to require information includes power to require any document which he believes may contain that information.

**Section 59**
*Interpretations.*

60.– (1) The purpose of this section is to ensure that so far as is possible (having regard to any relevant differences between the provisions concerned), questions arising under this Part in relation to competition within the United Kingdom are dealt with in a manner which is consistent with the treatment of corresponding questions arising in Community law in relation to competition within the Community.

(2) At any time when the court determines a question arising under this Part, it must act (so far as is compatible with the provisions of this Part and whether or not it would otherwise be required to do so) with a view to securing that there is no inconsistency between-

(a) the principles applied, and decision reached, by the court in determining that question; and

(b) the principles laid down by the Treaty and the European Court, and any relevant decision of that Court, as applicable at that time in determining any corresponding question arising in Community law.

(3) The court must, in addition, have regard to any relevant decision or statement of the Commission.

(4) Subsections (2) and (3) also apply to-

(a) the Director; and

(b) any person acting on behalf of the Director, in connection with any matter arising under this Part.

(5) In subsections (2) and (3), "court" means any court or tribunal.

(6) In subsections (2)(b) and (3), "decision" includes a decision as to-

(a) the interpretation of any provision of Community law;

(b) the civil liability of an undertaking for harm caused by its infringement of Community law.

**Section 60**
*This section sets out the important principles that will be applied in determining questions under Part I of the Act. The principles must, so far as is possible, be consistent with EC law.*

PART II

**Investigations in relation to Articles 85 and 86**

**61.**– (1) In this Part-

"Article 85" and

"Article 86" have the same meaning as in Part I;

"authorised officer", in relation to the Director, means an officer to whom an authorisation has been given under subsection (2);

"the Commission" means the European Commission;

"the Director" means the Director General of Fair Trading;

"Commission investigation" means an investigation ordered by a decision of the Commission under a prescribed provision of Community law relating to Article 85 or 86;

"Director's investigation" means an investigation conducted by the Director at the request of the Commission under a prescribed provision of Community law relating to Article 85 or 86;

"Director's special investigation" means a Director's investigation conducted at the request of the Commission in connection with a Commission investigation;

"prescribed" means prescribed by order made by the Secretary of State;

"premises" means-

(a) in relation to a Commission investigation, any premises, land or means of transport which an official of the Commission has power to enter in the course of the investigation; and

(b) in relation to a Director's investigation, any premises, land or means of transport which an official of the Commission would have power to enter if the investigation were being conducted by the Commission.

(2) For the purposes of a Director's investigation, an officer of the Director to whom an authorisation has been given has the powers of an official authorised by the Commission in connection with a Commission investigation under the relevant provision.

(3) "Authorisation" means an authorisation given in writing by the Director which-

(a) identifies the officer;
(b) specifies the subject matter and purpose of the investigation; and
(c) draws attention to any penalties which a person may incur in connection with the investigation under the relevant provision of Community law.

**Section 61**
*Definitions.*

**62.–** (1) A judge of the High Court may issue a warrant if satisfied, on an application made to the High Court in accordance with rules of court by the Director, that a Commission investigation is being, or is likely to be, obstructed.

**Section 62**
*S.62 enables the Director to apply to the High Court for a warrant that empowers him to enter premises. He may make the application when a European Commission investigation is 'being or is likely to be' obstructed.*

(2) A Commission investigation is being obstructed if-

    (a) an official of the Commission ("the Commission official"), exercising his power in accordance with the provision under which the investigation is being conducted, has attempted to enter premises but has been unable to do so; and

    (b) there are reasonable grounds for suspecting that there are books or records on the premises which the Commission official has power to examine.

(3) A Commission investigation is also being obstructed if there are reasonable grounds for suspecting that there are books or records on the premises-

    (a) the production of which has been required by an official of the Commission exercising his power in accordance with the provision under which the investigation is being conducted; and

    (b) which have not been produced as required.

**Section 62 (2) and (3)**
*The meaning of 'being obstructed'. See text.*

(4) A Commission investigation is likely to be obstructed if-

    (a) an official of the Commission ("the Commission official") is authorised for the purpose of the investigation;

    (b) there are reasonable grounds for suspecting that there are books or records on the premises which the Commission official has power to examine; and

(c) there are also reasonable grounds for suspecting that, if the Commission official attempted to exercise his power to examine any of the books or records, they would not be produced but would be concealed, removed, tampered with or destroyed.

**Section 62 (4) (a) to (c)**
*The meaning of 'likely to be obstructed'. See text.*

(5) A warrant under this section shall authorise-

(a) a named officer of the Director,
(b) any other of his officers whom he has authorised in writing to accompany the named officer, and
(c) any official of the Commission authorised for the purpose of the Commission investigation,

to enter the premises specified in the warrant, and search for books and records which the official has power to examine, using such force as is reasonably necessary for the purpose.

**Section 62 (5)**
*Further reference to the warrant. See also section 64.*

(6) Any person entering any premises by virtue of a warrant under this section may take with him such equipment as appears to him to be necessary.

(7) On leaving any premises entered by virtue of the warrant the named officer must, if the premises are unoccupied or the occupier is temporarily absent, leave them as effectively secured as he found them.

(8) A warrant under this section continues in force until the end of the period of one month beginning with the day on which it is issued.

(9) In the application of this section to Scotland, references to the High Court are to be read as references to the Court of Session.

**63.**– (1) A judge of the High Court may issue a warrant if satisfied, on an application made to the High Court in accordance with rules of court by the Director, that a Director's special investigation is being, or is likely to be, obstructed.

(2) A Director's special investigation is being obstructed if-

(a) an authorised officer of the Director has attempted to enter premises but has been unable to do so;

(b) the officer has produced his authorisation to the undertaking, or association of undertakings, concerned; and

(c) there are reasonable grounds for suspecting that there are books or records on the premises which the officer has power to examine.

(3) A Director's special investigation is also being obstructed if-

(a) there are reasonable grounds for suspecting that there are books or records on the premises which an authorised officer of the Director has power to examine;

(b) the officer has produced his authorisation to the undertaking, or association of undertakings, and has required production of the books or records; and

(c) the books and records have not been produced as required.

(4) A Director's special investigation is likely to be obstructed if-

(a) there are reasonable grounds for suspecting that there are books or records on the premises which an authorised officer of the Director has power to examine; and

(b) there are also reasonable grounds for suspecting that, if the officer attempted to exercise his power to examine any of the books or records, they would not be produced but would be concealed, removed, tampered with or destroyed.

(5) A warrant under this section shall authorise-

(a) a named authorised officer of the Director,

(b) any other authorised officer accompanying the named officer, and

(c) any named official of the Commission,

to enter the premises specified in the warrant, and search for books and records which the authorised officer has power to examine, using such force as is reasonably necessary for the purpose.

(6) Any person entering any premises by virtue of a warrant under this section may take with him such equipment as appears to him to be necessary.

(7) On leaving any premises which he has entered by virtue of the warrant the named officer must, if the premises are unoccupied or the occupier is temporarily absent, leave them as effectively secured as he found them.

(8) A warrant under this section continues in force until the end of the period of one month beginning with the day on which it is issued.

(9) In the application of this section to Scotland, references to the High Court are to be read as references to the Court of Session.

**Section 63**
*This section is similar to S. 62 but confers the powers of entry on the Director where he is conducting the actual investigation for the European Commission.*

**64.–** (1) A warrant issued under section 62 or 63 must indicate-

(a) the subject matter and purpose of the investigation;
(b) the nature of the offence created by section 65.

(2) The powers conferred by section 62 or 63 are to be exercised on production of a warrant issued under that section.

(3) If there is no one at the premises when the named officer proposes to execute such a warrant he must, before executing it-

(a) take such steps as are reasonable in all the circumstances to inform the occupier of the intended entry; and
(b) if the occupier is informed, afford him or his legal or other representative a reasonable opportunity to be present when the warrant is executed.

(4) If the named officer is unable to inform the occupier of the intended entry he must, when executing the warrant, leave a copy of it in a prominent place on the premises.

(5) In this section-

"named officer" means the officer named in the warrant; and

"occupier", in relation to any premises, means a person whom the named officer reasonably believes is the occupier of those premises.

**Section 64**
*This section details the requirements of the warrant. See also section 62(5).*

**65.–** (1) A person is guilty of an offence if he intentionally obstructs any person in the exercise of his powers under a warrant issued under section 62 or 63.

(2) A person guilty of an offence under subsection (1) is liable-

(a) on summary conviction, to a fine not exceeding the statutory maximum;
(b) on conviction on indictment, to imprisonment for a term not exceeding two years or to a fine or to both.

**Section 65**
*Obstruction of a person who is executing a warrant is a criminal offence.*

## PART III

### MONOPOLIES

**66.–** (1) Section 44 of the Fair Trading Act 1973 (power of the Director to require information about monopoly situations) is amended as follows.

(2) In subsection (1), for the words after paragraph (b) substitute-

"the Director may exercise the powers conferred by subsection (2) below for the purpose of assisting him in determining whether to take either of the following decisions with regard to that situation."

(3) After subsection (1) insert-

"(1A)  Those decisions are-

(a) whether to make a monopoly reference with respect to the existence or possible existence of the situation;
(b) whether, instead, to make a proposal under section 56A below for the Secretary of State to accept undertakings."

(4) For subsection (2) substitute-

"(2) In the circumstances and for the purpose mentioned in subsection (1) above, the Director may-

(a) require any person within subsection (3) below to produce to the Director, at a specified time and place-
(i)  any specified documents, or
(ii) any document which falls within a specified category,

which are in his custody or under his control and which are relevant;

(b) require any person within subsection (3) below who is carrying on a business to give the Director specified estimates, forecasts, returns, or other information, and specify the time at which and the form and manner in which the estimates, forecasts, returns or information are to be given;
(c) enter any premises used by a person within subsection (3) below for business purposes, and-
(i)  require any person on the premises to produce any documents on the premises which are in his custody or under his control and which are relevant;
(ii) require any person on the premises to give the Director such explanation of the documents as he may require.

(3) A person is within this subsection if-

(a) he produces goods of the description in question in the United Kingdom;
(b) he supplies goods or (as the case may be) services of the description in question in the United Kingdom; or
(c) such goods (or services) are supplied to him in the United Kingdom.

(4) The power to impose a requirement under subsection (2)(a) or (b) above is to be exercised by notice in writing served on the person on whom the requirement is imposed; and "specified" in those provisions means specified or otherwise described in the notice, and "specify" is to be read accordingly.

(5) The power under subsection (2)(a) above to require a person ("the person notified") to produce a document includes power-

    (a) if the document is produced-
        (i)  to take copies of it or extracts from it;
        (ii) to require the person notified, or any person who is a present or past officer of his, or is or was at any time employed by him, to provide an explanation of the document;

    (b) if the document is not produced, to require the person notified to state, to the best of his knowledge and belief, where it is.

(6) Nothing in this section confers power to compel any person-

    (a) to produce any document which he could not be compelled to produce in civil proceedings before the High Court or, in Scotland, the Court of Session; or

    (b) in complying with any requirement for the giving of information, to give any information which he could not be compelled to give in evidence in such proceedings.

(7) No person has to comply with a requirement imposed under subsection (2) above by a person acting under an authorisation under paragraph 7 of Schedule 1 to this Act unless evidence of the authorisation has, if required, been produced.

(8) For the purposes of subsection (2) above-

    (a) a document is relevant if-
        (i)  it is relevant to a decision mentioned in subsection (1A) above; and
        (ii) the powers conferred by this section are exercised in relation to the document for the purpose of assisting the Director in determining whether to take that decision;

    (b) "document" includes information recorded in any form; and

    (c) in relation to information recorded otherwise than in legible form, the power to require its production includes power to require production of it in legible form, so far as the means to do so are within the custody or under the control of the person on whom the requirement is imposed."

(5) The amendments made by this section and section 67 have effect in relation to sectoral regulators in accordance with paragraph 1 of Schedule 10.

**Section 66**
*This section extends the Directors powers in relation to investigating monopolies and amends the Fair Trading Act 1973.*

**67.**– (1) Section 46 of the Fair Trading Act 1973 is amended as follows.

(2) Omit subsections (1) and (2).

(3) At the end insert-

"(4) Any person who refuses or wilfully neglects to comply with a requirement imposed under section 44(2) above is guilty of an offence and liable-

    (a) on summary conviction, to a fine not exceeding the prescribed sum, or
    (b) on conviction on indictment, to imprisonment for a term not exceeding two years or to a fine or to both.

(5) If a person is charged with an offence under subsection (4) in respect of a requirement to produce a document, it is a defence for him to prove-

    (a) that the document was not in his possession or under his control; and
    (b) that it was not reasonably practicable for him to comply with the requirement.

(6) If a person is charged with an offence under subsection (4) in respect of a requirement-

    (a) to provide an explanation of a document, or
    (b) to state where a document is to be found,

it is a defence for him to prove that he had a reasonable excuse for failing to comply with the requirement.

(7) A person who intentionally obstructs the Director in the exercise of his powers under section 44 is guilty of an offence and liable-

    (a) on summary conviction, to a fine not exceeding the prescribed sum;
    (b) on conviction on indictment, to a fine.

(8) A person who wilfully alters, suppresses or destroys any document which he has been required to produce under section 44(2) is guilty of an offence and liable-

    (a) on summary conviction, to a fine not exceeding the prescribed sum;
    (b) on conviction on indictment, to imprisonment for a term not exceeding two years or to a fine or to both."

**Section 67**

*This section amends S.46 of the Fair Trading Act 1973 and increases penalties for persons who refuse or wilfully neglect to comply with S. 44(2) of the Act.*

**68.** In section 137 of the Fair Trading Act 1973, after subsection (3) insert-

"(3A) The Secretary of State may by order made by statutory instrument-

(a) provide that "the supply of services" in the provisions of this Act is to include, or to cease to include, any activity specified in the order which consists in, or in making arrangements in connection with, permitting the use of land; and

(b) for that purpose, amend or repeal any of paragraphs (c), (d), (e) or (g) of subsection (3) above.

(3B) No order under subsection (3A) above is to be made unless a draft of the order has been laid before Parliament and approved by a resolution of each House of Parliament.

(3C) The provisions of Schedule 9 to this Act apply in the case of a draft of any such order as they apply in the case of a draft of an order to which section 91(1) above applies."

## Section 68
*This section inserts a provision into the Fair Trading Act 1973 concerning services relating to the use of land.*

69. In section 83 of the Fair Trading Act 1973-

(a) in subsection (1), omit "Subject to subsection (1A) below"; and

(b) omit subsection (1A) (reports on monopoly references to be transmitted to certain persons at least twenty-four hours before laying before Parliament).

## Section 69
*This section makes changes to the Patents Act 1977.*

PART IV

SUPPLEMENTAL AND TRANSITIONAL

70. Sections 44 and 45 of the Patents Act 1977 shall cease to have effect.

71.– (1) Any power to make regulations or orders which is conferred by this Act is exercisable by statutory instrument.

(2) The power to make rules which is conferred by section 48 is exercisable by statutory instrument.

(3) Any statutory instrument made under this Act may-

(a) contain such incidental, supplemental, consequential and transitional provision as the Secretary of State considers appropriate; and

(b) make different provision for different cases.

(4) No order is to be made under-

    (a) section 3,
    (b) section 19,
    (c) section 36(8),
    (d) section 50, or
    (e) paragraph 6(3) of Schedule 4,

unless a draft of the order has been laid before Parliament and approved by a resolution of each House.

(5) Any statutory instrument made under this Act, apart from one made-

    (a) under any of the provisions mentioned in subsection (4), or
    (b) under section 76(3),

shall be subject to annulment by a resolution of either House of Parliament.

## Section 71

*This section refers to the provision of regulations, orders and rules by way of statutory instrument.*

**72.–** (1) This section applies to an offence under any of sections 42 to 44, 55(8) or 65.

(2) If an offence committed by a body corporate is proved-

    (a) to have been committed with the consent or connivance of an officer, or
    (b) to be attributable to any neglect on his part,

the officer as well as the body corporate is guilty of the offence and liable to be proceeded against and punished accordingly.

(3) In subsection (2) "officer", in relation to a body corporate, means a director, manager, secretary or other similar officer of the body, or a person purporting to act in any such capacity.

(4) If the affairs of a body corporate are managed by its members, subsection (2) applies in relation to the acts and defaults of a member in connection with his functions of management as if he were a director of the body corporate.

(5) If an offence committed by a partnership in Scotland is proved-

    (a) to have been committed with the consent or connivance of a partner, or
    (b) to be attributable to any neglect on his part,

the partner as well as the partnership is guilty of the offence and liable to be proceeded against and punished accordingly.

(6) In subsection (5) "partner" includes a person purporting to act as a partner.

**Section 72**
*This section deals with the application of offences to bodies corporate.*

**73.**– (1) Any provision made by or under this Act binds the Crown except that-

(a) the Crown is not criminally liable as a result of any such provision;

(b) the Crown is not liable for any penalty under any such provision; and

(c) nothing in this Act affects Her Majesty in her private capacity.

(2) Subsection (1)(a) does not affect the application of any provision of this Act in relation to persons in the public service of the Crown.

(3) Subsection (1)(c) is to be interpreted as if section 38(3) of the Crown Proceedings Act 1947 (interpretation of references in that Act to Her Majesty in her private capacity) were contained in this Act.

(4) If, in respect of a suspected infringement of the Chapter I prohibition or of the Chapter II prohibition otherwise than by the Crown or a person in the public service of the Crown, an investigation is conducted under section 25-

(a) the power conferred by section 27 may not be exercised in relation to land which is occupied by a government department, or otherwise for purposes of the Crown, without the written consent of the appropriate person; and

(b) section 28 does not apply in relation to land so occupied.

(5) In any case in which consent is required under subsection (4), the person who is the appropriate person in relation to that case is to be determined in accordance with regulations made by the Secretary of State.

(6) Sections 62 and 63 do not apply in relation to land which is occupied by a government department, or otherwise for purposes of the Crown, unless the matter being investigated is a suspected infringement by the Crown or by a person in the public service of the Crown.

(7) In subsection (6) "infringement" means an infringement of Community law relating to Article 85 or 86 of the Treaty establishing the European Community.

(8) If the Secretary of State certifies that it appears to him to be in the interests of national security that the powers of entry-

(a) conferred by section 27, or

(b) that may be conferred by a warrant under section 28, 62 or 63,

should not be exercisable in relation to premises held or used by or on behalf of the Crown and which are specified in the certificate, those powers are not exercisable in relation to those premises.

(9) Any amendment, repeal or revocation made by this Act binds the Crown to the extent that the enactment amended, repealed or revoked binds the Crown.

**Section 73**
*This section refers to the application of this Act on the State.*

74.– (1) The minor and consequential amendments set out in Schedule 12 are to have effect.

(2) The transitional provisions and savings set out in Schedule 13 are to have effect.

(3) The enactments set out in Schedule 14 are repealed.

**Section 74**
*Schedules 12,13 and 14 deal with minor and consequential amendments, transitional provisions and the repeal of certain enactment's.*

75.– (1) The Secretary of State may by order make such incidental, consequential, transitional or supplemental provision as he thinks necessary or expedient for the general purposes, or any particular purpose, of this Act or in consequence of any of its provisions or for giving full effect to it.

(2) An order under subsection (1) may, in particular, make provision-

    (a) for enabling any person by whom any powers will become exercisable, on a date specified by or under this Act, by virtue of any provision made by or under this Act to take before that date any steps which are necessary as a preliminary to the exercise of those powers;

    (b) for making savings, or additional savings, from the effect of any repeal made by or under this Act.

(3) Amendments made under this section shall be in addition, and without prejudice, to those made by or under any other provision of this Act.

(4) No other provision of this Act restricts the powers conferred by this section.

**Section 75**
*This section enables the Secretary of State to make incidental, consequential, transitional or supplemental provisions.*

76.– (1) This Act may be cited as the Competition Act 1998.

(2) Sections 71 and 75 and this section and paragraphs 1 to 7 and 35 of Schedule 13 come into force on the passing of this Act.

(3) The other provisions of this Act come into force on such day as the Secretary of State may by order appoint; and different days may be appointed for different purposes.

(4) This Act extends to Northern Ireland.

# SCHEDULES

## SCHEDULE 1

EXCLUSIONS: MERGERS AND CONCENTRATIONS

PART I

MERGERS

### Enterprises ceasing to be distinct: the Chapter I prohibition

**1.–** (1) To the extent to which an agreement (either on its own or when taken together with another agreement) results, or if carried out would result, in any two enterprises ceasing to be distinct enterprises for the purposes of Part V of the Fair Trading Act 1973 ("the 1973 Act"), the Chapter I prohibition does not apply to the agreement.

(2) The exclusion provided by sub-paragraph (1) extends to any provision directly related and necessary to the implementation of the merger provisions.

(3) In sub-paragraph (2) "merger provisions" means the provisions of the agreement which cause, or if carried out would cause, the agreement to have the result mentioned in sub-paragraph (1).

(4) Section 65 of the 1973 Act applies for the purposes of this paragraph as if-

 (a) in subsection (3) (circumstances in which a person or group of persons may be treated as having control of an enterprise), and
 (b) in subsection (4) (circumstances in which a person or group of persons may be treated as bringing an enterprise under their control),

for "may" there were substituted "must".

### Enterprises ceasing to be distinct: the Chapter II prohibition

**2.–** (1) To the extent to which conduct (either on its own or when taken together with other conduct)-

 (a) results in any two enterprises ceasing to be distinct enterprises for the purposes of Part V of the 1973 Act), or
 (b) is directly related and necessary to the attainment of the result mentioned in paragraph (a),

the Chapter II prohibition does not apply to that conduct.

(2) Section 65 of the 1973 Act applies for the purposes of this paragraph as it applies for the purposes of paragraph 1.

## Transfer of a newspaper or of newspaper assets

**3.**– (1) The Chapter I prohibition does not apply to an agreement to the extent to which it constitutes, or would if carried out constitute, a transfer of a newspaper or of newspaper assets for the purposes of section 57 of the 1973 Act.

(2) The Chapter II prohibition does not apply to conduct (either on its own or when taken together with other conduct) to the extent to which-

(a) it constitutes such a transfer, or
(b) it is directly related and necessary to the implementation of the transfer.

(3) The exclusion provided by sub-paragraph (1) extends to any provision directly related and necessary to the implementation of the transfer.

## Withdrawal of the paragraph 1 exclusion

**4.**– (1) The exclusion provided by paragraph 1 does not apply to a particular agreement if the Director gives a direction under this paragraph to that effect.

(2) If the Director is considering whether to give a direction under this paragraph, he may by notice in writing require any party to the agreement in question to give him such information in connection with the agreement as he may require.

(3) The Director may give a direction under this paragraph only as provided in sub-paragraph (4) or (5).

(4) If at the end of such period as may be specified in rules under section 51 a person has failed, without reasonable excuse, to comply with a requirement imposed under sub-paragraph (2), the Director may give a direction under this paragraph.

(5) The Director may also give a direction under this paragraph if-

(a) he considers-
   (i)  that the agreement will, if not excluded, infringe the Chapter I prohibition; and
   (ii) that he is not likely to grant it an unconditional individual exemption; and
(b) the agreement is not a protected agreement.

(6) For the purposes of sub-paragraph (5), an individual exemption is unconditional if no conditions or obligations are imposed in respect of it under section 4(3)(a).

(7) A direction under this paragraph-

(a) must be in writing;
(b) may be made so as to have effect from a date specified in the direction (which may not be earlier than the date on which it is given).

## Protected agreements

**5.**  An agreement is a protected agreement for the purposes of paragraph 4 if-

(a) the Secretary of State has announced his decision not to make a merger reference to the Competition Commission under section 64 of the 1973 Act in connection with the agreement;

(b) the Secretary of State has made a merger reference to the Competition Commission under section 64 of the 1973 Act in connection with the agreement and the Commission has found that the agreement has given rise to, or would if carried out give rise to, a merger situation qualifying for investigation;

(c) the agreement does not fall within sub-paragraph (a) or (b) but has given rise to, or would if carried out give rise to, enterprises to which it relates being regarded under section 65 of the 1973 Act as ceasing to be distinct enterprises (otherwise than as the result of subsection (3) or (4)(b) of that section); or

(d) the Secretary of State has made a merger reference to the Competition Commission under section 32 of the Water Industry Act 1991 in connection with the agreement and the Commission has found that the agreement has given rise to, or would if carried out give rise to, a merger of the kind to which that section applies.

## PART II

### CONCENTRATIONS SUBJECT TO EC CONTROLS

**6.**– (1) To the extent to which an agreement (either on its own or when taken together with another agreement) gives rise to, or would if carried out give rise to, a concentration, the Chapter I prohibition does not apply to the agreement if the Merger Regulation gives the Commission exclusive jurisdiction in the matter.

(2) To the extent to which conduct (either on its own or when taken together with other conduct) gives rise to, or would if pursued give rise to, a concentration, the Chapter II prohibition does not apply to the conduct if the Merger Regulation gives the Commission exclusive jurisdiction in the matter.

(3) In this paragraph-

"concentration" means a concentration with a Community dimension within the meaning of Articles 1 and 3 of the Merger Regulation; and

"Merger Regulation" means Council Regulation (EEC) No. 4064/89 of 21st December 1989 on the control of concentrations between undertakings as amended by Council Regulation (EC) No. 1310/97 of 30th June 1997.

## SCHEDULE 2

EXCLUSIONS: OTHER COMPETITION SCRUTINY

## PART I

FINANCIAL SERVICES

### The Financial Services Act 1986 (c.60)

**1.**– (1) The Financial Services Act 1986 is amended as follows.

(2) For section 125 (effect of the Restrictive Trade Practices Act 1976), substitute-

**125.**– (1) The Chapter I prohibition does not apply to an agreement for the constitution of-

(a) a recognised self-regulating organisation,
(b) a recognised investment exchange, or
(c) a recognised clearing house,

to the extent to which the agreement relates to the regulating provisions of the body concerned.

(2) Subject to subsection (3) below, the Chapter I prohibition does not apply to an agreement for the constitution of-

(a) a self-regulating organisation,
(b) an investment exchange, or
(c) a clearing house,

to the extent to which the agreement relates to the regulating provisions of the body concerned.

(3) The exclusion provided by subsection (2) above applies only if-

(a) the body has applied for a recognition order in accordance with the provisions of this Act; and
(b) the application has not been determined.

(4) The Chapter I prohibition does not apply to a decision made by-

(a) a recognised self-regulating organisation,
(b) a recognised investment exchange, or
(c) a recognised clearing house,

to the extent to which the decision relates to any of that body's regulating provisions or specified practices.

(5) The Chapter I prohibition does not apply to the specified practices of-

(a) a recognised self-regulating organisation, a recognised investment exchange or a recognised clearing house; or
(b) a person who is subject to-
    (i) the rules of one of those bodies, or

(ii) the statements of principle, rules, regulations or codes of practice made by a designated agency in the exercise of functions transferred to it by a delegation order.

(6) The Chapter I prohibition does not apply to any agreement the parties to which consist of or include-

(a) a recognised self-regulating organisation, a recognised investment exchange or a recognised clearing house; or
(b) a person who is subject to-
    (i) the rules of one of those bodies, or
    (ii) the statements of principle, rules, regulations or codes of practice made by a designated agency in the exercise of functions transferred to it by a delegation order,

to the extent to which the agreement consists of provisions the inclusion of which is required or contemplated by any of the body's regulating provisions or specified practices or by the statements of principle, rules, regulations or codes of practice of the agency.

(7) The Chapter I prohibition does not apply to-

(a) any clearing arrangements; or
(b) any agreement between a recognised investment exchange and a recognised clearing house, to the extent to which the agreement consists of provisions the inclusion of which in the agreement is required or contemplated by any clearing arrangements.

(8) If the recognition order in respect of a body of the kind mentioned in subsection (1)(a), (b) or (c) above is revoked, subsections (1) and (4) to (7) above are to have effect as if that body had continued to be recognised until the end of the period of six months beginning with the day on which the revocation took effect.

(9) In this section-

"the Chapter I prohibition" means the prohibition imposed by section 2(1) of the Competition Act 1998;

"regulating provisions" means-

(a) in relation to a self-regulating organisation, any rules made, or guidance issued, by the organisation;
(b) in relation to an investment exchange, any rules made, or guidance issued, by the exchange;
(c) in relation to a clearing house, any rules made, or guidance issued, by the clearing house;

"specified practices" means-

(a) in the case of a recognised self-regulating organisation, the practices mentioned in section 119(2)(a)(ii) and (iii) above (read with section 119(5) and (6)(a));

(b) in the case of a recognised investment exchange, the practices mentioned in section 119(2)(b)(ii) and (iii) above (read with section 119(5) and (6)(b));

(c) in the case of a recognised clearing house, the practices mentioned in section 119(2)(c)(ii) and (iii) above (read with section 119(5) and (6)(b));

(d) in the case of a person who is subject to the statements of principle, rules, regulations or codes of practice issued or made by a designated agency in the exercise of functions transferred to it by a delegation order, the practices mentioned in section 121(2)(c) above (read with section 121(4));

and expressions used in this section which are also used in Part I of the Competition Act 1998 are to be interpreted in the same way as for the purposes of that Part of that Act."

(3) Omit section 126 (certain practices not to constitute anti-competitive practices for the purposes of the Competition Act 1980).

(4) For section 127 (modification of statutory provisions in relation to recognised professional bodies), substitute-

**127.**– (1) This section applies to-

(a) any agreement for the constitution of a recognised professional body to the extent to which it relates to the rules or guidance of that body relating to the carrying on of investment business by persons certified by it ("investment business rules"); and

(b) any other agreement, the parties to which consist of or include-

(i) a recognised professional body,

(ii) a person certified by such a body, or

(iii) a member of such a body,

and which contains a provision required or contemplated by that body's investment business rules.

(2) If it appears to the Treasury, in relation to some or all of the provisions of an agreement to which this section applies-

(a) that the provisions in question do not have, and are not intended or likely to have, to any significant extent the effect of restricting, distorting or preventing competition; or

(b) that the effect of restricting, distorting or preventing competition which the provisions in question do have, or are intended or are likely to have, is not greater than is necessary for the protection of investors,

the Treasury may make a declaration to that effect.

(3) If the Treasury make a declaration under this section, the Chapter I prohibition does not apply to the agreement to the extent to which the agreement consists of provisions to which the declaration relates.

(4) If the Treasury are satisfied that there has been a material change of circumstances, they may-

    (a) revoke a declaration made under this section, if they consider that the grounds on which it was made no longer exist;

    (b) vary such a declaration, if they consider that there are grounds for making a different declaration; or

    (c) make a declaration even though they have notified the Director of their intention not to do so.

(5) If the Treasury make, vary or revoke a declaration under this section they must notify the Director of their decision.

(6) If the Director proposes to exercise any Chapter III powers in respect of any provisions of an agreement to which this section applies, he must-

    (a) notify the Treasury of his intention to do so; and

    (b) give the Treasury particulars of the agreement and such other information-

        (i) as he considers will assist the Treasury to decide whether to exercise their powers under this section; or

        (ii) as the Treasury may request.

(7) The Director may not exercise his Chapter III powers in respect of any provisions of an agreement to which this section applies, unless the Treasury-

    (a) have notified him that they have not made a declaration in respect of those provisions under this section and that they do not intend to make such a declaration; or

    (b) have revoked a declaration under this section and a period of six months beginning with the date on which the revocation took effect has expired.

(8) A declaration under this section ceases to have effect if the agreement to which it relates ceases to be one to which this section applies.

(9) In this section-

"the Chapter I prohibition" means the prohibition imposed by section 2(1) of the Competition Act 1998,

"Chapter III powers" means the powers given to the Director by Chapter III of Part I of that Act so far as they relate to the Chapter I prohibition, and

expressions used in this section which are also used in Part I of the Competition Act 1998 are to be interpreted in the same way as for the purposes of that Part of that Act.

(10) In this section references to an agreement are to be read as applying equally to, or in relation to, a decision or concerted practice.

(11) In the application of this section to decisions and concerted practices, references to provisions of an agreement are to be read as references to elements of a decision or concerted practice."

Part II

Companies

**The Companies Act 1989 (c.40)**

**2.–** (1) The Companies Act 1989 is amended as follows.

(2) In Schedule 14, for paragraph 9 (exclusion of certain agreements from the Restrictive Trade Practices Act 1976), substitute-

**"The Competition Act 1998**

**9.–** (1) The Chapter I prohibition does not apply to an agreement for the constitution of a recognised supervisory or qualifying body to the extent to which it relates to-

(a) rules of, or guidance issued by, the body; and
(b) incidental matters connected with the rules or guidance.

(2) The Chapter I prohibition does not apply to an agreement the parties to which consist of or include-

(a) a recognised supervisory or qualifying body, or
(b) any person mentioned in paragraph 3(5) or (6) above,

to the extent to which the agreement consists of provisions the inclusion of which in the agreement is required or contemplated by the rules or guidance of that body.

(3) The Chapter I prohibition does not apply to the practices mentioned in paragraph 3(4)(a) and (b) above.

(4) Where a recognition order is revoked, sub-paragraphs (1) to (3) above are to continue to apply for a period of six months beginning with the day on which the revocation takes effect, as if the order were still in force.

(5) In this paragraph-

(a) "the Chapter I prohibition" means the prohibition imposed by section 2(1) of the Competition Act 1998,
(b) references to an agreement are to be read as applying equally to, or in relation to, a decision or concerted practice,

and expressions used in this paragraph which are also used in Part I of the Competition Act 1998 are to be interpreted in the same way as for the purposes of that Part of that Act.

(6) In the application of this paragraph to decisions and concerted practices, references to provisions of an agreement are to be read as references to elements of a decision or concerted practice."

**The Companies (Northern Ireland) Order 1990 (S.I. 1990/593 (N.I. 5))**

**3.–** (1) The Companies (Northern Ireland) Order 1990 is amended as follows.

(2) In Schedule 14, for paragraph 9 (exclusion of certain agreements from the Restrictive Trade Practices Act 1976), substitute-

**"The Competition Act 1998**

**9.**– (1) The Chapter I prohibition does not apply to an agreement for the constitution of a recognised supervisory or qualifying body to the extent to which it relates to-

(a) rules of, or guidance issued by, the body; and
(b) incidental matters connected with the rules or guidance.

(2) The Chapter I prohibition does not apply to an agreement the parties to which consist of or include-

(a) a recognised supervisory or qualifying body, or
(b) any person mentioned in paragraph 3(5) or (6),

to the extent to which the agreement consists of provisions the inclusion of which in the agreement is required or contemplated by the rules or guidance of that body.

(3) The Chapter I prohibition does not apply to the practices mentioned in paragraph 3(4)(a) and (b).

(4) Where a recognition order is revoked, sub-paragraphs (1) to (3) are to continue to apply for a period of 6 months beginning with the day on which the revocation takes effect, as if the order were still in force.

(5) In this paragraph-

(a) "the Chapter I prohibition" means the prohibition imposed by section 2(1) of the Competition Act 1998,
(b) references to an agreement are to be read as applying equally to, or in relation to, a decision or concerted practice,

and expressions used in this paragraph which are also used in Part I of the Competition Act 1998 are to be interpreted in the same way as for the purposes of that Part of that Act.

(6) In the application of this paragraph to decisions and concerted practices, references to provisions of an agreement are to be read as references to elements of a decision or concerted practice."

PART III

BROADCASTING

**The Broadcasting Act 1990 (c.42)**

**4.**– (1) The Broadcasting Act 1990 is amended as follows.

(2) In section 194A (which modifies the Restrictive Trade Practices Act 1976 in its application to agreements relating to Channel 3 news provision), for subsections (2) to (6), substitute-

"(2) If, having sought the advice of the Director, it appears to the Secretary of State, in relation to some or all of the provisions of a relevant agreement, that the conditions mentioned in subsection (3) are satisfied, he may make a declaration to that effect.

(3) The conditions are that-

  (a) the provisions in question do not have, and are not intended or likely to have, to any significant extent the effect of restricting, distorting or preventing competition; or
  (b) the effect of restricting, distorting or preventing competition which the provisions in question do have or are intended or are likely to have, is not greater than is necessary-
    (i) in the case of a relevant agreement falling within subsection (1)(a), for securing the appointment by holders of regional Channel 3 licences of a single body corporate to be the appointed news provider for the purposes of section 31(2), or
    (ii) in the case of a relevant agreement falling within subsection (1)(b), for compliance by them with conditions included in their licences by virtue of section 31(1) and (2).

(4) If the Secretary of State makes a declaration under this section, the Chapter I prohibition does not apply to the agreement to the extent to which the agreement consists of provisions to which the declaration relates.

(5) If the Secretary of State is satisfied that there has been a material change of circumstances, he may-

  (a) revoke a declaration made under this section, if he considers that the grounds on which it was made no longer exist;
  (b) vary such a declaration, if he considers that there are grounds for making a different declaration; or
  (c) make a declaration, even though he has notified the Director of his intention not to do so.

(6) If the Secretary of State makes, varies or revokes a declaration under this section, he must notify the Director of his decision.

(7) The Director may not exercise any Chapter III powers in respect of a relevant agreement, unless-

  (a) he has notified the Secretary of State of his intention to do so; and
  (b) the Secretary of State-
    (i) has notified the Director that he has not made a declaration in respect of the agreement, or provisions of the agreement, under this section and that he does not intend to make such a declaration; or

(ii) has revoked a declaration under this section and a period of six months beginning with the date on which the revocation took effect has expired.

(8) If the Director proposes to exercise any Chapter III powers in respect of a relevant agreement, he must give the Secretary of State particulars of the agreement and such other information-

(a) as he considers will assist the Secretary of State to decide whether to exercise his powers under this section; or

(b) as the Secretary of State may request.

(9) In this section-

"the Chapter I prohibition" means the prohibition imposed by section 2(1) of the Competition Act 1998;

"Chapter III powers" means the powers given to the Director by Chapter III of Part I of that Act so far as they relate to the Chapter I prohibition;

"Director" means the Director General of Fair Trading;

"regional Channel 3 licence" has the same meaning as in Part I;

and expressions used in this section which are also used in Part I of the Competition Act 1998 are to be interpreted in the same way as for the purposes of that Part of that Act.

(10) In this section references to an agreement are to be read as applying equally to, or in relation to, a decision or concerted practice.

(11) In the application of this section to decisions and concerted practices, references to provisions of an agreement are to be read as references to elements of a decision or concerted practice."

## Networking arrangements under the Broadcasting Act 1990 (c.42)

5.– (1) The Chapter I prohibition does not apply in respect of any networking arrangements to the extent to which they-

(a) are subject to Schedule 4 to the Broadcasting Act 1990 (competition references with respect to networking arrangements); or

(b) contain provisions which have been considered under that Schedule.

(2) The Independent Television Commission ("ITC") must publish a list of the networking arrangements which in their opinion are excluded from the Chapter I prohibition by virtue of sub-paragraph (1).

(3) The ITC must-

(a) consult the Director before publishing the list, and

(b) publish the list in such a way as they think most suitable for bringing it to the attention of persons who, in their opinion, would be affected by, or likely to have an interest in, it.

(4) In this paragraph "networking arrangements" means-

(a) any arrangements entered into as mentioned in section 39(4) or (7)(b) of the Broadcasting Act 1990, or

(b) any agreements-

(i) which do not constitute arrangements of the kind mentioned in paragraph (a), but

(ii) which are made for the purpose mentioned in section 39(1) of that Act, or

(c) any modification of the arrangements or agreements mentioned in paragraph (a) or (b).

## PART IV

### ENVIRONMENTAL PROTECTION

**Producer responsibility obligations**

**6.**– (1) The Environment Act 1995 is amended as follows.

(2) In section 94(1) (supplementary provisions about regulations imposing producer responsibility obligations on prescribed persons), after paragraph (o), insert-

"(oa) the exclusion or modification of any provision of Part I of the Competition Act 1998 in relation to exemption schemes or in relation to any agreement, decision or concerted practice at least one of the parties to which is an operator of an exemption scheme;".

(3) After section 94(6), insert-

"(6A) Expressions used in paragraph (oa) of subsection (1) above which are also used in Part I of the Competition Act 1998 are to be interpreted in the same way as for the purposes of that Part of that Act."

(4) After section 94, insert-

**94A.**– (1) For the purposes of this section, the relevant paragraphs are paragraphs (n), (o), (oa) and (ya) of section 94(1) above.

(2) Regulations made by virtue of any of the relevant paragraphs may include transitional provision in respect of agreements or exemption schemes-

(a) in respect of which information has been required for the purposes of competition scrutiny under any regulation made by virtue of paragraph (ya);

(b) which are being, or have been, considered for the purposes of competition scrutiny under any regulation made by virtue of paragraph (n) or (ya); or

(c) in respect of which provisions of the Restrictive Trade Practices Acts 1976 and 1977 have been modified or excluded in accordance with any regulation made by virtue of paragraph (o).

(3) Subsections (2), (3), (5) to (7) and (10) of section 93 above do not apply to a statutory instrument which contains only regulations made by virtue of any of the relevant paragraphs or subsection (2) above.

(4) Such a statutory instrument shall be subject to annulment in pursuance of a resolution of either House of Parliament."

# SCHEDULE 3
## GENERAL EXCLUSIONS

**Planning obligations**

1.– (1) The Chapter I prohibition does not apply to an agreement-

(a) to the extent to which it is a planning obligation;
(b) which is made under section 75 (agreements regulating development or use of land) or 246 (agreements relating to Crown land) of the Town and Country Planning (Scotland) Act 1997; or
(c) which is made under Article 40 of the Planning (Northern Ireland) Order 1991.

(2) In sub-paragraph (1)(a), "planning obligation" means-

(a) a planning obligation for the purposes of section 106 of the Town and Country Planning Act 1990; or
(b) a planning obligation for the purposes of section 299A of that Act.

**Section 21(2) agreements**

2.– (1) The Chapter I prohibition does not apply to an agreement in respect of which a direction under section 21(2) of the (1976 c. 34.)Restrictive Trade Practices Act 1976 is in force immediately before the coming into force of section 2 ("a section 21(2) agreement").

(2) If a material variation is made to a section 21(2) agreement, sub-paragraph (1) ceases to apply to the agreement on the coming into force of the variation.

(3) Sub-paragraph (1) does not apply to a particular section 21(2) agreement if the Director gives a direction under this paragraph to that effect.

(4) If the Director is considering whether to give a direction under this paragraph, he may by notice in writing require any party to the agreement in question to give him such information in connection with the agreement as he may require.

(5) The Director may give a direction under this paragraph only as provided in sub-paragraph (6) or (7).

(6) If at the end of such period as may be specified in rules under section 51 a person has failed, without reasonable excuse, to comply with a requirement imposed under sub-paragraph (4), the Director may give a direction under this paragraph.

(7) The Director may also give a direction under this paragraph if he considers-

(a) that the agreement will, if not excluded, infringe the Chapter I prohibition; and

(b) that he is not likely to grant it an unconditional individual exemption.

(8) For the purposes of sub-paragraph (7) an individual exemption is unconditional if no conditions or obligations are imposed in respect of it under section 4(3)(a).

(9) A direction under this paragraph-

(a) must be in writing;

(b) may be made so as to have effect from a date specified in the direction (which may not be earlier than the date on which it is given).

## EEA Regulated Markets

**3.**– (1) The Chapter I prohibition does not apply to an agreement for the constitution of an EEA regulated market to the extent to which the agreement relates to any of the rules made, or guidance issued, by that market.

(2) The Chapter I prohibition does not apply to a decision made by an EEA regulated market, to the extent to which the decision relates to any of the market's regulating provisions.

(3) The Chapter I prohibition does not apply to-

(a) any practices of an EEA regulated market; or

(b) any practices which are trading practices in relation to an EEA regulated market.

(4) The Chapter I prohibition does not apply to an agreement the parties to which are or include-

(a) an EEA regulated market, or

(b) a person who is subject to the rules of that market,

to the extent to which the agreement consists of provisions the inclusion of which is required or contemplated by the regulating provisions of that market.

(5) In this paragraph-

"EEA regulated market" is a market which-

(a) is listed by an EEA State other than the United Kingdom pursuant to article 16 of Council Directive No. 93/22/EEC of 10th May 1993 on investment services in the securities field; and

(b) operates without any requirement that a person dealing on the market should have a physical presence in the EEA State from which any trading facilities are provided or on any trading floor that the market may have;

"EEA State" means a State which is a contracting party to the EEA Agreement;

"regulating provisions", in relation to an EEA regulated market, means-

(a) rules made, or guidance issued, by that market,
(b) practices of that market, or
(c) practices which, in relation to that market, are trading practices;

"trading practices", in relation to an EEA regulated market, means practices of persons who are subject to the rules made by that market, and-

(a) which relate to business in respect of which those persons are subject to the rules of that market, and which are required or contemplated by those rules or by guidance issued by that market; or
(b) which are otherwise attributable to the conduct of that market as such.

### Services of general economic interest etc.

4.   Neither the Chapter I prohibition nor the Chapter II prohibition applies to an undertaking entrusted with the operation of services of general economic interest or having the character of a revenue-producing monopoly in so far as the prohibition would obstruct the performance, in law or in fact, of the particular tasks assigned to that undertaking.

### Compliance with legal requirements

5.– (1) The Chapter I prohibition does not apply to an agreement to the extent to which it is made in order to comply with a legal requirement.

(2) The Chapter II prohibition does not apply to conduct to the extent to which it is engaged in an order to comply with a legal requirement.

(3) In this paragraph "legal requirement" means a requirement-

(a) imposed by or under any enactment in force in the United Kingdom;
(b) imposed by or under the Treaty or the EEA Agreement and having legal effect in the United Kingdom without further enactment; or
(c) imposed by or under the law in force in another Member State and having legal effect in the United Kingdom.

### Avoidance of conflict with international obligations

6.– (1) If the Secretary of State is satisfied that, in order to avoid a conflict between provisions of this Part and an international obligation of the United Kingdom, it would be appropriate for the Chapter I prohibition not to apply to-

(a) a particular agreement, or
(b) any agreement of a particular description,

he may by order exclude the agreement, or agreements of that description, from the Chapter I prohibition.

(2) An order under sub-paragraph (1) may make provision for the exclusion of the agreement or agreements to which the order applies, or of such of them as may be specified, only in specified circumstances.

(3) An order under sub-paragraph (1) may also provide that the Chapter I prohibition is to be deemed never to have applied in relation to the agreement or agreements, or in relation to such of them as may be specified.

(4) If the Secretary of State is satisfied that, in order to avoid a conflict between provisions of this Part and an international obligation of the United Kingdom, it would be appropriate for the Chapter II prohibition not to apply in particular circumstances, he may by order provide for it not to apply in such circumstances as may be specified.

(5) An order under sub-paragraph (4) may provide that the Chapter II prohibition is to be deemed never to have applied in relation to specified conduct.

(6) An international arrangement relating to civil aviation and designated by an order made by the Secretary of State is to be treated as an international obligation for the purposes of this paragraph.

(7) In this paragraph and paragraph 7 "specified" means specified in the order.

## Public policy

7.– (1) If the Secretary of State is satisfied that there are exceptional and compelling reasons of public policy why the Chapter I prohibition ought not to apply to-

(a) a particular agreement, or
(b) any agreement of a particular description,

he may by order exclude the agreement, or agreements of that description, from the Chapter I prohibition.

(2) An order under sub-paragraph (1) may make provision for the exclusion of the agreement or agreements to which the order applies, or of such of them as may be specified, only in specified circumstances.

(3) An order under sub-paragraph (1) may also provide that the Chapter I prohibition is to be deemed never to have applied in relation to the agreement or agreements, or in relation to such of them as may be specified.

(4) If the Secretary of State is satisfied that there are exceptional and compelling reasons of public policy why the Chapter II prohibition ought not to apply in particular circumstances, he may by order provide for it not to apply in such circumstances as may be specified.

(5) An order under sub-paragraph (4) may provide that the Chapter II prohibition is to be deemed never to have applied in relation to specified conduct.

### Coal and steel

8.– (1) The Chapter I prohibition does not apply to an agreement which relates to a coal or steel product to the extent to which the ECSC Treaty gives the Commission exclusive jurisdiction in the matter.

(2) Sub-paragraph (1) ceases to have effect on the date on which the ECSC Treaty expires ("the expiry date").

(3) The Chapter II prohibition does not apply to conduct which relates to a coal or steel product to the extent to which the ECSC Treaty gives the Commission exclusive jurisdiction in the matter.

(4) Sub-paragraph (3) ceases to have effect on the expiry date.

(5) In this paragraph-

"coal or steel product" means any product of a kind listed in Annex I to the ECSC Treaty; and

"ECSC Treaty" means the Treaty establishing the European Coal and Steel Community.

### Agricultural products

9.– (1) The Chapter I prohibition does not apply to an agreement to the extent to which it relates to production of or trade in an agricultural product and-

(a) forms an integral part of a national market organisation;
(b) is necessary for the attainment of the objectives set out in Article 39 of the Treaty; or
(c) is an agreement of farmers or farmers' associations (or associations of such associations) belonging to a single member State which concerns-
  (i)  the production or sale of agricultural products, or
  (ii) the use of joint facilities for the storage, treatment or processing of agricultural products,

and under which there is no obligation to charge identical prices.

(2) If the Commission determines that an agreement does not fulfil the conditions specified by the provision for agricultural products for exclusion from Article 85(1), the exclusion provided by this paragraph ("the agriculture exclusion") is to be treated as ceasing to apply to the agreement on the date of the decision.

(3) The agriculture exclusion does not apply to a particular agreement if the Director gives a direction under this paragraph to that effect.

(4) If the Director is considering whether to give a direction under this paragraph, he may by notice in writing require any party to the agreement in question to give him such information in connection with the agreement as he may require.

(5) The Director may give a direction under this paragraph only as provided in sub-paragraph (6) or (7).

(6) If at the end of such period as may be specified in rules under section 51 a person has failed, without reasonable excuse, to comply with a requirement imposed under sub-paragraph (4), the Director may give a direction under this paragraph.

(7) The Director may also give a direction under this paragraph if he considers that an agreement (whether or not he considers that it infringes the Chapter I prohibition) is likely, or is intended, substantially and unjustifiably to prevent, restrict or distort competition in relation to an agricultural product.

(8) A direction under this paragraph-

(a) must be in writing;
(b) may be made so as to have effect from a date specified in the direction (which may not be earlier than the date on which it is given).

(9) In this paragraph-

"agricultural product" means any product of a kind listed in Annex II to the Treaty; and

"provision for agricultural products" means Council Regulation (EEC) No. 26/62 of 4th April 1962 applying certain rules of competition to production of and trade in agricultural products.

SCHEDULE 4

PROFESSIONAL RULES

PART I

EXCLUSION

**General**

**1.**- (1) To the extent to which an agreement (either on its own or when taken together with another agreement)-

(a) constitutes a designated professional rule,
(b) imposes obligations arising from designated professional rules, or
(c) constitutes an agreement to act in accordance with such rules,

the Chapter I prohibition does not apply to the agreement.

(2) In this Schedule-

"designated" means designated by the Secretary of State under paragraph 2;

"professional rules" means rules regulating a professional service or the persons providing, or wishing to provide, that service;

"professional service" means any of the services described in Part II of this Schedule; and

"rules" includes regulations, codes of practice and statements of principle.

### Designated rules

2.– (1) The Secretary of State must establish and maintain a list designating, for the purposes of this Schedule, rules-

(a) which are notified to him under paragraph 3; and
(b) which, in his opinion, are professional rules.

(2) The list is to be established, and any alteration in the list is to be effected, by an order made by the Secretary of State.

(3) The designation of any rule is to have effect from such date (which may be earlier than the date on which the order listing it is made) as may be specified in that order.

### Application for designation

3.– (1) Any body regulating a professional service or the persons who provide, or wish to provide, that service may apply to the Secretary of State for rules of that body to be designated.

(2) An application under this paragraph must-

(a) be accompanied by a copy of the rules to which it relates; and
(b) be made in the prescribed manner.

### Alterations

4.– (1) A rule does not cease to be a designated professional rule merely because it is altered.

(2) If such a rule is altered (whether by being modified, revoked or replaced), the body concerned must notify the Secretary of State and the Director of the alteration as soon as is reasonably practicable.

### Reviewing the list

5.– (1) The Secretary of State must send to the Director-

(a) a copy of any order made under paragraph 2; and

(b) a copy of the professional rules to which the order relates.

(2) The Director must-

(a) retain any copy of a professional rule which is sent to him under sub-paragraph (1)(b) so long as the rule remains in force;

(b) maintain a copy of the list, as altered from time to time; and

(c) keep the list under review.

(3) If the Director considers-

(a) that, with a view to restricting the exclusion provided by this Schedule, some or all of the rules of a particular body should no longer be designated, or

(b) that rules which are not designated should be designated,

he must advise the Secretary of State accordingly.

## Removal from the list

**6.**– (1) This paragraph applies if the Secretary of State receives advice under paragraph 5(3)(a).

(2) If it appears to the Secretary of State that another Minister of the Crown has functions in relation to the professional service concerned, he must consult that Minister.

(3) If it appears to the Secretary of State, having considered the Director's advice and the advice of any other Minister resulting from consultation under sub-paragraph (2), that the rules in question should no longer be designated, he may by order revoke their designation.

(4) Revocation of a designation is to have effect from such date as the order revoking it may specify.

## Inspection

**7.**– (1) Any person may inspect, and take a copy of-

(a) any entry in the list of designated professional rules as kept by the Director under paragraph 5(2); or

(b) any copy of professional rules retained by him under paragraph 5(1).

(2) The right conferred by sub-paragraph (1) is to be exercised only-

(a) at a time which is reasonable;

(b) on payment of such fee as the Director may determine; and

(c) at such offices of his as the Director may direct.

# PART II

## PROFESSIONAL SERVICES

**Legal**

8. The services of barristers, advocates or solicitors.

**Medical**

9. The provision of medical or surgical advice or attendance and the performance of surgical operations.

**Dental**

10. Any services falling within the practice of dentistry within the meaning of the Dentists Act 1984.

**Ophthalmic**

11. The testing of sight.

**Veterinary**

12. Any services which constitute veterinary surgery within the meaning of the Veterinary Surgeons Act 1966.

**Nursing**

13. The services of nurses.

**Midwifery**

14. The services of midwives.

**Physiotherapy**

15. The services of physiotherapists.

**Chiropody**

16. The services of chiropodists.

**Architectural**

17. The services of architects.

**Accounting and auditing**

18. The making or preparation of accounts or accounting records and the examination, verification and auditing of financial statements.

## Insolvency

**19.** Insolvency services within the meaning of section 428 of the Insolvency Act 1986.

## Patent agency

**20.** The services of registered patent agents (within the meaning of Part V of the Copyright, Designs and Patents Act 1988).

**21.** The services of persons carrying on for gain in the United Kingdom the business of acting as agents or other representatives for or obtaining European patents or for the purpose of conducting proceedings in relation to applications for or otherwise in connection with such patents before the European Patent Office or the comptroller and whose names appear on the European list (within the meaning of Part V of the Copyright, Designs and Patents Act 1988).

## Parliamentary agency

**22.** The services of parliamentary agents entered in the register in either House of Parliament as agents entitled to practise both in promoting and in opposing Bills.

## Surveying

**23.** The services of surveyors of land, of quantity surveyors, of surveyors of buildings or other structures and of surveyors of ships.

## Engineering and technology etc.

**24.** The services of persons practising or employed as consultants in the field of-

    (a) civil engineering;
    (b) mechanical, aeronautical, marine, electrical or electronic engineering;
    (c) mining, quarrying, soil analysis or other forms of mineralogy or geology;
    (d) agronomy, forestry, livestock rearing or ecology;
    (e) metallurgy, chemistry, biochemistry or physics; or
    (f) any other form of engineering or technology analogous to those mentioned in sub-paragraphs (a) to (e).

## Educational

**25.** The provision of education or training.

## Religious

**26.** The services of ministers of religion.

## SCHEDULE 5

### Notification under Chapter I: Procedure

**Terms used**

1. In this Schedule-

   "applicant" means the person making an application to which this Schedule applies;

   "application" means an application under section 13 or an application under section 14;

   "application for guidance" means an application under section 13;

   "application for a decision" means an application under section 14;

   "rules" means rules made by the Director under section 51; and

   "specified" means specified in the rules.

**General rules about applications**

2.– (1) An application must be made in accordance with rules.

(2) A party to an agreement who makes an application must take all reasonable steps to notify all other parties to the agreement of whom he is aware-

   (a) that the application has been made; and
   (b) as to whether it is for guidance or a decision.

(3) Notification under sub-paragraph (2) must be in the specified manner.

**Preliminary investigation**

3.– (1) If, after a preliminary investigation of an application, the Director considers that it is likely-

   (a) that the agreement concerned will infringe the Chapter I prohibition, and
   (b) that it would not be appropriate to grant the agreement an individual exemption,

he may make a decision ("a provisional decision") under this paragraph.

(2) If the Director makes a provisional decision-

   (a) the Director must notify the applicant in writing of his provisional decision; and
   (b) section 13(4) or (as the case may be) section 14(4) is to be taken as never having applied.

(3) When making a provisional decision, the Director must follow such procedure as may be specified.

(4) A provisional decision does not affect the final determination of an application.

(5) If the Director has given notice to the applicant under sub-paragraph (2) in respect of an application for a decision, he may continue with the application under section 14.

## Procedure on application for guidance

**4.** When determining an application for guidance, the Director must follow such procedure as may be specified.

## Procedure on application for a decision

**5.**– (1) When determining an application for a decision, the Director must follow such procedure as may be specified.

(2) The Director must arrange for the application to be published in such a way as he thinks most suitable for bringing it to the attention of those likely to be affected by it, unless he is satisfied that it will be sufficient for him to seek information from one or more particular persons other than the applicant.

(3) In determining the application, the Director must take into account any representations made to him by persons other than the applicant.

## Publication of decisions

**6.** If the Director determines an application for a decision he must publish his decision, together with his reasons for making it, in such manner as may be specified.

## Delay by the Director

**7.**– (1) This paragraph applies if the court is satisfied, on the application of a person aggrieved by the failure of the Director to determine an application for a decision in accordance with the specified procedure, that there has been undue delay on the part of the Director in determining the application.

(2) The court may give such directions to the Director as it considers appropriate for securing that the application is determined without unnecessary further delay.

## SCHEDULE 6

NOTIFICATION UNDER CHAPTER II: PROCEDURE

## Terms used

**1.** In this Schedule–

"applicant" means the person making an application to which this Schedule applies;

"application" means an application under section 21 or an application under section 22;

"application for guidance" means an application under section 21;

"application for a decision" means an application under section 22;

"other party", in relation to conduct of two or more persons, means one of those persons other than the applicant;

"rules" means rules made by the Director under section 51; and

"specified" means specified in the rules.

### General rules about applications

**2.–** (1) An application must be made in accordance with rules.

(2) If the conduct to which an application relates is conduct of two or more persons, the applicant must take all reasonable steps to notify all of the other parties of whom he is aware-

(a) that the application has been made; and
(b) as to whether it is for guidance or a decision.

(3) Notification under sub-paragraph (2) must be in the specified manner.

### Preliminary investigation

**3.–** (1) If, after a preliminary investigation of an application, the Director considers that it is likely that the conduct concerned will infringe the Chapter II prohibition, he may make a decision ("a provisional decision") under this paragraph.

(2) If the Director makes a provisional decision, he must notify the applicant in writing of that decision.

(3) When making a provisional decision, the Director must follow such procedure as may be specified.

(4) A provisional decision does not affect the final determination of an application.

(5) If the Director has given notice to the applicant under sub-paragraph (2) in respect of an application for a decision, he may continue with the application under section 22.

### Procedure on application for guidance

**4.** When determining an application for guidance, the Director must follow such procedure as may be specified.

## Procedure on application for a decision

5.– (1) When determining an application for a decision, the Director must follow such procedure as may be specified.

(2) The Director must arrange for the application to be published in such a way as he thinks most suitable for bringing it to the attention of those likely to be affected by it, unless he is satisfied that it will be sufficient for him to seek information from one or more particular persons other than the applicant.

(3) In determining the application, the Director must take into account any representations made to him by persons other than the applicant.

## Publication of decisions

6. If the Director determines an application for a decision he must publish his decision, together with his reasons for making it, in such manner as may be specified.

## Delay by the Director

7.– (1) This paragraph applies if the court is satisfied, on the application of a person aggrieved by the failure of the Director to determine an application for a decision in accordance with the specified procedure, that there has been undue delay on the part of the Director in determining the application.

(2) The court may give such directions to the Director as it considers appropriate for securing that the application is determined without unnecessary further delay.

SCHEDULE 7

THE COMPETITION COMMISSION

PART I

GENERAL

## Interpretation

1. In this Schedule-

"the 1973 Act" means the Fair Trading Act 1973;

"appeal panel member" means a member appointed under paragraph 2(1)(a);

"Chairman" means the chairman of the Commission;

"the Commission" means the Competition Commission;

"Council" has the meaning given in paragraph 5;

"general functions" means any functions of the Commission other than functions-

(a) in connection with appeals under this Act; or

(b) which are to be discharged by the Council;

"member" means a member of the Commission;

"newspaper merger reference" means a newspaper merger reference under section 59 of the 1973 Act;

"President" has the meaning given by paragraph 4(2);

"reporting panel member" means a member appointed under paragraph 2(1)(b);

"secretary" means the secretary of the Commission appointed under paragraph 9; and

"specialist panel member" means a member appointed under any of the provisions mentioned in paragraph 2(1)(d).

**Membership of the Commission**

**2.**– (1) The Commission is to consist of-

(a) members appointed by the Secretary of State to form a panel for the purposes of the Commission's functions in relation to appeals;

(b) members appointed by the Secretary of State to form a panel for the purposes of the Commission's general functions;

(c) members appointed (in accordance with paragraph 15(5)) from the panel maintained under paragraph 22;

(d) members appointed by the Secretary of State under or by virtue of-

(i) section 12(4) or 14(8) of the Water Industry Act 1991;

(ii) section 12(9) of the Electricity Act 1989;

(iii) section 13(10) of the Telecommunications Act 1984;

(iv) Article 15(9) of the Electricity (Northern Ireland) Order 1992.

(2) A person who is appointed as a member of a kind mentioned in one of paragraphs (a) to (c) of sub-paragraph (3) may also be appointed as a member of either or both of the other kinds mentioned in those paragraphs.

(3) The kinds of member are-

(a) an appeal panel member;

(b) a reporting panel member;

(c) a specialist panel member.

(4) Before appointing a person who is qualified for appointment to the panel of chairmen (see paragraph 26(2)), the Secretary of State must consult the Lord Chancellor or Lord Advocate, as he considers appropriate.

(5) The validity of the Commission's proceedings is not affected by a defect in the appointment of a member.

## Chairman and deputy chairmen

**3.**– (1) The Commission is to have a chairman appointed by the Secretary of State from among the reporting panel members.

(2) The Secretary of State may appoint one or more of the reporting panel members to act as deputy chairman.

(3) The Chairman, and any deputy chairman, may resign that office at any time by notice in writing addressed to the Secretary of State.

(4) If the Chairman (or a deputy chairman) ceases to be a member he also ceases to be Chairman (or a deputy chairman).

(5) If the Chairman is absent or otherwise unable to act, or there is no chairman, any of his functions may be performed-

    (a) if there is one deputy chairman, by him;

    (b) if there is more than one-

        (i) by the deputy chairman designated by the Secretary of State; or

        (ii) if no such designation has been made, by the deputy chairman designated by the deputy chairmen;

    (c) if there is no deputy chairman able to act-

        (i) by the member designated by the Secretary of State; or

        (ii) if no such designation has been made, by the member designated by the Commission.

## President

**4.**– (1) The Secretary of State must appoint one of the appeal panel members to preside over the discharge of the Commission's functions in relation to appeals.

(2) The member so appointed is to be known as the President of the Competition Commission Appeal Tribunals (but is referred to in this Schedule as "the President").

(3) The Secretary of State may not appoint a person to be the President unless that person-

    (a) has a ten year general qualification within the meaning of section 71 of the Courts and Legal Services Act 1990,

    (b) is an advocate or solicitor in Scotland of at least ten years' standing, or

    (c) is-

        (i) a member of the Bar of Northern Ireland of at least ten years' standing, or

        (ii) a solicitor of the Supreme Court of Northern Ireland of at least ten years' standing,

and appears to the Secretary of State to have appropriate experience and knowledge of competition law and practice.

(4) Before appointing the President, the Secretary of State must consult the Lord Chancellor or Lord Advocate, as he considers appropriate.

(5) If the President ceases to be a member he also ceases to be President.

## The Council

5.– (1) The Commission is to have a management board to be known as the Competition Commission Council (but referred to in this Schedule as "the Council").

(2) The Council is to consist of-

(a) the Chairman;
(b) the President;
(c) such other members as the Secretary of State may appoint; and
(d) the secretary.

(3) In exercising its functions under paragraphs 3 and 7 to 12 and paragraph 5 of Schedule 8, the Commission is to act through the Council.

(4) The Council may determine its own procedure including, in particular, its quorum.

(5) The Chairman (and any person acting as Chairman) is to have a casting vote on any question being decided by the Council.

## Term of office

6.– (1) Subject to the provisions of this Schedule, each member is to hold and vacate office in accordance with the terms of his appointment.

(2) A person is not to be appointed as a member for more than five years at a time.

(3) Any member may at any time resign by notice in writing addressed to the Secretary of State.

(4) The Secretary of State may remove a member on the ground of incapacity or misbehaviour.

(5) No person is to be prevented from being appointed as a member merely because he has previously been a member.

## Expenses, remuneration and pensions

7.– (1) The Secretary of State shall pay to the Commission such sums as he considers appropriate to enable it to perform its functions.

(2) The Commission may pay, or make provision for paying, to or in respect of each member such salaries or other remuneration and such pensions, allowances, fees, expenses or gratuities as the Secretary of State may determine.

(3) If a person ceases to be a member otherwise than on the expiry of his term of office and it appears to the Secretary of State that there are special circumstances which make it right for him to receive compensation, the Commission may make a payment to him of such amount as the Secretary of State may determine.

(4) The approval of the Treasury is required for-

(a) any payment under sub-paragraph (1);

(b) any determination of the Secretary of State under sub-paragraph (2) or (3).

### The Commission's powers

8. Subject to the provisions of this Schedule, the Commission has power to do anything (except borrow money)-

(a) calculated to facilitate the discharge of its functions; or

(b) incidental or conducive to the discharge of its functions.

### Staff

9.– (1) The Commission is to have a secretary, appointed by the Secretary of State on such terms and conditions of service as he considers appropriate.

(2) The approval of the Treasury is required as to those terms and conditions.

(3) Before appointing a person to be secretary, the Secretary of State must consult the Chairman and the President.

(4) Subject to obtaining the approval of-

(a) the Secretary of State, as to numbers, and

(b) the Secretary of State and Treasury, as to terms and conditions of service,

the Commission may appoint such staff as it thinks appropriate.

### Procedure

10. Subject to any provision made by or under this Act, the Commission may regulate its own procedure.

### Application of seal and proof of instruments

11.– (1) The application of the seal of the Commission must be authenticated by the signature of the secretary or of some other person authorised for the purpose.

(2) Sub-paragraph (1) does not apply in relation to any document which is or is to be signed in accordance with the law of Scotland.

(3) A document purporting to be duly executed under the seal of the Commission-

(a) is to be received in evidence; and

(b) is to be taken to have been so executed unless the contrary is proved.

**Accounts**

**12.**– (1) The Commission must-

  (a) keep proper accounts and proper records in relation to its accounts;

  (b) prepare a statement of accounts in respect of each of its financial years; and

  (c) send copies of the statement to the Secretary of State and to the Comptroller and Auditor General before the end of the month of August next following the financial year to which the statement relates.

(2) The statement of accounts must comply with any directions given by the Secretary of State with the approval of the Treasury as to-

  (a) the information to be contained in it,

  (b) the manner in which the information contained in it is to be presented, or

  (c) the methods and principles according to which the statement is to be prepared,

and must contain such additional information as the Secretary of State may with the approval of the Treasury require to be provided for informing Parliament.

(3) The Comptroller and Auditor General must-

  (a) examine, certify and report on each statement received by him as a result of this paragraph; and

  (b) lay copies of each statement and of his report before each House of Parliament.

(4) In this paragraph "financial year" means the period beginning with the date on which the Commission is established and ending with March 31st next, and each successive period of twelve months.

**Status**

**13.**– (1) The Commission is not to be regarded as the servant or agent of the Crown or as enjoying any status, privilege or immunity of the Crown.

(2) The Commission's property is not to be regarded as property of, or held on behalf of, the Crown.

PART II

PERFORMANCE OF THE COMMISSION'S GENERAL FUNCTIONS

**Interpretation**

**14.** In this Part of this Schedule "group" means a group selected under paragraph 15.

**Discharge of certain functions by groups**

**15.**– (1) Except where sub-paragraph (7) gives the Chairman power to act on his own, any general function of the Commission must be performed through a group selected for the purpose by the Chairman.

(2) The group must consist of at least three persons one of whom may be the Chairman.

(3) In selecting the members of the group, the Chairman must comply with any requirement as to its constitution imposed by any enactment applying to specialist panel members.

(4) If the functions to be performed through the group relate to a newspaper merger reference, the group must, subject to sub-paragraph (5), consist of such reporting panel members as the Chairman may select.

(5) The Secretary of State may appoint one, two or three persons from the panel maintained under paragraph 22 to be members and, if he does so, the group-

    (a) must include that member or those members; and

    (b) if there are three such members, may (if the Chairman so decides) consist entirely of those members.

(6) Subject to sub-paragraphs (2) to (5), a group must consist of reporting panel members or specialist panel members selected by the Chairman.

(7) While a group is being constituted to perform a particular general function of the Commission, the Chairman may-

    (a) take such steps (falling within that general function) as he considers appropriate to facilitate the work of the group when it has been constituted; or

    (b) exercise the power conferred by section 75(5) of the 1973 Act (setting aside references).

## Chairmen of groups

**16.** The Chairman must appoint one of the members of a group to act as the chairman of the group.

## Replacement of member of group

**17.**– (1) If, during the proceedings of a group-

    (a) a member of the group ceases to be a member of the Commission,

    (b) the Chairman is satisfied that a member of the group will be unable for a substantial period to perform his duties as a member of the group, or

    (c) it appears to the Chairman that because of a particular interest of a member of the group it is inappropriate for him to remain in the group,

the Chairman may appoint a replacement.

(2) The Chairman may also at any time appoint any reporting panel member to be an additional member of a group.

**Attendance of other members**

**18.–** (1) At the invitation of the chairman of a group, any reporting panel member who is not a member of the group may attend meetings or otherwise take part in the proceedings of the group.

(2) But any person attending in response to such an invitation may not-

    (a) vote in any proceedings of the group; or

    (b) have a statement of his dissent from a conclusion of the group included in a report made by them.

(3) Nothing in sub-paragraph (1) is to be taken to prevent a group, or a member of a group, from consulting any member of the Commission with respect to any matter or question with which the group is concerned.

**Procedure**

**19.–** (1) Subject to any special or general directions given by the Secretary of State, each group may determine its own procedure.

(2) Each group may, in particular, determine its quorum and determine-

    (a) the extent, if any, to which persons interested or claiming to be interested in the subject-matter of the reference are allowed-

        (i) to be present or to be heard, either by themselves or by their representatives;

        (ii) to cross-examine witnesses; or

        (iii) otherwise to take part; and

    (b) the extent, if any, to which sittings of the group are to be held in public.

(3) In determining its procedure a group must have regard to any guidance issued by the Chairman.

(4) Before issuing any guidance for the purposes of this paragraph the Chairman must consult the members of the Commission.

**Effect of exercise of functions by group**

**20.–** (1) Subject to sub-paragraph (2), anything done by or in relation to a group in, or in connection with, the performance of functions to be performed by the group is to have the same effect as if done by or in relation to the Commission.

(2) For the purposes of-

    (a) sections 56 and 73 of the 1973 Act,

    (b) section 19A of the (1958 c. 47.)Agricultural Marketing Act 1958,

    (c) Articles 23 and 42 of the Agricultural Marketing (Northern Ireland) Order 1982,

a conclusion contained in a report of a group is to be disregarded if the conclusion is not that of at least two-thirds of the members of the group.

## Casting votes

**21.** The chairman of a group is to have a casting vote on any question to be decided by the group.

## Newspaper merger references

**22.** The Secretary of State must maintain a panel of persons whom he regards as suitable for selection as members of a group constituted in connection with a newspaper merger reference.

PART III

APPEALS

## Interpretation

**23.** In this Part of this Schedule-

"panel of chairmen" means the panel appointed under paragraph 26; and

"tribunal" means an appeal tribunal constituted in accordance with paragraph 27.

## Training of appeal panel members

**24.** The President must arrange such training for appeal panel members as he considers appropriate.

## Acting President

**25.** If the President is absent or otherwise unable to act, the Secretary of State may appoint as acting president an appeal panel member who is qualified to act as chairman of a tribunal.

## Panel of tribunal chairmen

**26.**– (1) There is to be a panel of appeal panel members appointed by the Secretary of State for the purposes of providing chairmen of appeal tribunals established under this Part of this Schedule.

(2) A person is qualified for appointment to the panel of chairmen only if-

    (a) he has a seven year general qualification within the meaning of section 71 of the Courts and Legal Services Act 1990,

    (b) he is an advocate or solicitor in Scotland of at least seven years' standing, or

    (c) he is-

        (i) a member of the Bar of Northern Ireland of at least seven years' standing, or

        (ii) a solicitor of the Supreme Court of Northern Ireland of at least seven years' standing,

and appears to the Secretary of State to have appropriate experience and knowledge of competition law and practice.

## Constitution of tribunals

**27.**– (1) On receipt of a notice of appeal, the President must constitute an appeal tribunal to deal with the appeal.

(2) An appeal tribunal is to consist of-

    (a) a chairman, who must be either the President or a person appointed by him to be chairman from the panel of chairmen; and

    (b) two other appeal panel members appointed by the President.

## PART IV

### MISCELLANEOUS

## Disqualification of members for House of Commons

**28.** In Part II of Schedule 1 to the House of Commons Disqualification Act 1975 (bodies of which all members are disqualified) insert at the appropriate place-

"The Competition Commission".

## Disqualification of members for Northern Ireland Assembly

**29.** In Part II of Schedule 1 to the Northern Ireland Assembly Disqualification Act 1975 (bodies of which all members are disqualified) insert at the appropriate place-

"The Competition Commission".

## PART V

### TRANSITIONAL PROVISIONS

## Interpretation

**30.** In this Part of this Schedule-

"commencement date" means the date on which section 45 comes into force; and

"MMC" means the Monopolies and Mergers Commission.

## Chairman

**31.**– (1) The person who is Chairman of the MMC immediately before the commencement date is on that date to become both a member of the Commission and its chairman as if he had been duly appointed under paragraphs 2(1)(b) and 3.

(2) He is to hold office as Chairman of the Commission for the remainder of the period for which he was appointed as Chairman of the MMC and on the terms on which he was so appointed.

## Deputy chairmen

**32.** The persons who are deputy chairmen of the MMC immediately before the commencement date are on that date to become deputy chairmen of the Commission as if they had been duly appointed under paragraph 3(2).

## Reporting panel members

**33.– (1)** The persons who are members of the MMC immediately before the commencement date are on that date to become members of the Commission as if they had been duly appointed under paragraph 2(1)(b).

(2) Each of them is to hold office as a member for the remainder of the period for which he was appointed as a member of the MMC and on the terms on which he was so appointed.

## Specialist panel members

**34.– (1)** The persons who are members of the MMC immediately before the commencement date by virtue of appointments made under any of the enactments mentioned in paragraph 2(1)(d) are on that date to become members of the Commission as if they had been duly appointed to the Commission under the enactment in question.

(2) Each of them is to hold office as a member for such period and on such terms as the Secretary of State may determine.

## Secretary

**35.** The person who is the secretary of the MMC immediately before the commencement date is on that date to become the secretary of the Commission as if duly appointed under paragraph 9, on the same terms and conditions.

## Council

**36.– (1)** The members who become deputy chairmen of the Commission under paragraph 32 are also to become members of the Council as if they had been duly appointed under paragraph 5(2)(c).

(2) Each of them is to hold office as a member of the Council for such period as the Secretary of State determines.

SCHEDULE 8

APPEALS

PART I

GENERAL

## Interpretation

**1.** In this Schedule-

"the chairman" means a person appointed as chairman of a tribunal in accordance with paragraph 27(2)(a) of Schedule 7;

"the President" means the President of the Competition Commission Appeal Tribunals appointed under paragraph 4 of Schedule 7;

"rules" means rules made by the Secretary of State under section 48;

"specified" means specified in rules;

"tribunal" means an appeal tribunal constituted in accordance with paragraph 27 of Schedule 7.

## General procedure

**2.**– (1) An appeal to the Competition Commission must be made by sending a notice of appeal to the Commission within the specified period.

(2) The notice of appeal must set out the grounds of appeal in sufficient detail to indicate-

(a) under which provision of this Act the appeal is brought;
(b) to what extent (if any) the appellant contends that the decision against, or with respect to which, the appeal is brought was based on an error of fact or was wrong in law; and
(c) to what extent (if any) the appellant is appealing against the Director's exercise of his discretion in making the disputed decision.

(3) The tribunal may give an appellant leave to amend the grounds of appeal identified in the notice of appeal.

## Decisions of the tribunal

**3.**– (1) The tribunal must determine the appeal on the merits by reference to the grounds of appeal set out in the notice of appeal.

(2) The tribunal may confirm or set aside the decision which is the subject of the appeal, or any part of it, and may-

(a) remit the matter to the Director,
(b) impose or revoke, or vary the amount of, a penalty,

(c) grant or cancel an individual exemption or vary any conditions or obligations imposed in relation to the exemption by the Director,

(d) give such directions, or take such other steps, as the Director could himself have given or taken, or

(e) make any other decision which the Director could himself have made.

(3) Any decision of the tribunal on an appeal has the same effect, and may be enforced in the same manner, as a decision of the Director.

(4) If the tribunal confirms the decision which is the subject of the appeal it may nevertheless set aside any finding of fact on which the decision was based.

**4.–** (1) A decision of the tribunal may be taken by a majority.

(2) The decision must-

(a) state whether it was unanimous or taken by a majority; and

(b) be recorded in a document which-

(i)  contains a statement of the reasons for the decision; and

(ii) is signed and dated by the chairman of the tribunal.

(3) When the tribunal is preparing the document mentioned in sub-paragraph (2)(b), section 56 is to apply to the tribunal as it applies to the Director.

(4) The President must make such arrangements for the publication of the tribunal's decision as he considers appropriate.

PART II

RULES

**Registrar of Appeal Tribunals**

**5.–** (1) Rules may provide for the appointment by the Competition Commission, with the approval of the Secretary of State, of a Registrar of Appeal Tribunals.

(2) The rules may, in particular-

(a) specify the qualifications for appointment as Registrar; and

(b) provide for specified functions relating to appeals to be exercised by the Registrar in specified circumstances.

**Notice of appeal**

**6.** Rules may make provision-

(a) as to the period within which appeals must be brought;

(b) as to the form of the notice of appeal and as to the information which must be given in the notice;

(c) with respect to amendment of a notice of appeal;

(d) with respect to acknowledgement of a notice of appeal.

**Response to the appeal**

7. Rules may provide for the tribunal to reject an appeal if-

   (a) it considers that the notice of appeal reveals no valid ground of appeal; or
   (b) it is satisfied that the appellant has habitually and persistently and without any reasonable ground-
      (i) instituted vexatious proceedings, whether against the same person or against different persons; or
      (ii) made vexatious applications in any proceedings.

**Pre-hearing reviews and preliminary matters**

8.– (1) Rules may make provision-

   (a) for the carrying-out by the tribunal of a preliminary consideration of proceedings (a "pre-hearing review"); and
   (b) for enabling such powers to be exercised in connection with a pre-hearing review as may be specified.

(2) If rules make provision of the kind mentioned in sub-paragraph (1), they may also include-

   (a) provision for security; and
   (b) supplemental provision.

(3) In sub-paragraph (2) "provision for security" means provision authorising a tribunal carrying out a pre-hearing review under the rules, in specified circumstances, to make an order requiring a party to the proceedings, if he wishes to continue to participate in them, to pay a deposit of an amount not exceeding such sum-

   (a) as may be specified; or
   (b) as may be calculated in accordance with specified provisions.

(4) In sub-paragraph (2) "supplemental provision" means any provision as to-

   (a) the manner in which the amount of such a deposit is to be determined;
   (b) the consequences of non-payment of such a deposit; and
   (c) the circumstances in which any such deposit, or any part of it, may be-
      (i) refunded to the person who paid it; or
      (ii) paid to another party to the proceedings.

**Conduct of the hearing**

9.– (1) Rules may make provision-

   (a) as to the manner in which appeals are to be conducted, including provision for any hearing to be held in private if the tribunal considers it appropriate because it may be considering information of a kind to which section 56 applies;

(b) as to the persons entitled to appear on behalf of the parties;

(c) for requiring persons to attend to give evidence and produce documents and for authorising the administration of oaths to witnesses;

(d) as to the evidence which may be required or admitted in proceedings before the tribunal and the extent to which it should be oral or written;

(e) allowing the tribunal to fix time limits with respect to any aspect of the proceedings before it and to extend any time limit (whether or not it has expired);

(f) for enabling the tribunal to refer a matter back to the Director if it appears to the tribunal that the matter has not been adequately investigated;

(g) for enabling the tribunal, on the application of any party to the proceedings before it or on its own initiative-
   (i) in England and Wales or Northern Ireland, to order the disclosure between, or the production by, the parties of documents or classes of documents;
   (ii) in Scotland, to order such recovery or inspection of documents as might be ordered by a sheriff;

(h) for the appointment of experts for the purposes of any proceedings before the tribunal;

(i) for the award of costs or expenses, including any allowances payable to persons in connection with their attendance before the tribunal;

(j) for taxing or otherwise settling any costs or expenses directed to be paid by the tribunal and for the enforcement of any such direction.

(2) A person who without reasonable excuse fails to comply with-

(a) any requirement imposed by virtue of sub-paragraph (1)(c), or

(b) any requirement with respect to the disclosure, production, recovery or inspection of documents which is imposed by virtue of sub-paragraph (1)(g),

is guilty of an offence and liable on summary conviction to a fine not exceeding level 3 on the standard scale.

### Interest

**10.–** (1) Rules may make provision-

(a) as to the circumstances in which the tribunal may order that interest is payable;

(b) for the manner in which and the periods by reference to which interest is to be calculated and paid.

(2) The rules may, in particular, provide that compound interest is to be payable if the tribunal-

(a) upholds a decision of the Director to impose a penalty, or

(b) does not reduce a penalty so imposed by more than a specified percentage,

but in such a case the rules may not provide that interest is to be payable in respect of any period before the date on which the appeal was brought.

**Fees**

**11.**– (1) Rules may provide-

(a) for fees to be chargeable in respect of specified costs of proceedings before the tribunal;

(b) for the amount of such costs to be determined by the tribunal.

(2) Any sums received in consequence of rules under this paragraph are to be paid into the Consolidated Fund.

**Withdrawing an appeal**

**12.** Rules may make provision-

(a) that a party who has brought an appeal may not withdraw it without the leave of-
  (i) the tribunal, or
  (ii) in specified circumstances, the President or the Registrar;

(b) for the tribunal to grant leave to withdraw the appeal on such conditions as it considers appropriate;

(c) enabling the tribunal to publish any decision which it could have made had the appeal not been withdrawn;

(d) as to the effect of withdrawal of an appeal;

(e) as to any procedure to be followed if parties to proceedings on an appeal agree to settle.

**Interim orders**

**13.**– (1) Rules may provide for the tribunal to make an order ("an interim order") granting, on an interim basis, any remedy which the tribunal would have power to grant in its final decision.

(2) An interim order may, in particular, suspend the effect of a decision made by the Director or vary the conditions or obligations attached to an exemption.

(3) Rules may also make provision giving the tribunal powers similar to those given to the Director by section 35.

**Miscellaneous**

**14.** Rules may make provision-

(a) for a person who is not a party to proceedings on an appeal to be joined in those proceedings;

(b) for appeals to be consolidated on such terms as the tribunal thinks appropriate in such circumstances as may be specified.

## SCHEDULE 9
### DIRECTOR'S RULES

**General**

1. In this Schedule-

    "application for guidance" means an application for guidance under section 13 or 21;

    "application for a decision" means an application for a decision under section 14 or 22;

    "guidance" means guidance given under section 13 or 21;

    "rules" means rules made by the Director under section 51; and

    "specified" means specified in rules.

**Applications**

2. Rules may make provision-

    (a) as to the form and manner in which an application for guidance or an application for a decision must be made;
    (b) for the procedure to be followed in dealing with the application;
    (c) for the application to be dealt with in accordance with a timetable;
    (d) as to the documents and information which must be given to the Director in connection with the application;
    (e) requiring the applicant to give such notice of the application, to such other persons, as may be specified;
    (f) as to the consequences of a failure to comply with any rule made by virtue of sub-paragraph (e);
    (g) as to the procedure to be followed when the application is subject to the concurrent jurisdiction of the Director and a regulator.

**Provisional decisions**

3. Rules may make provision as to the procedure to be followed by the Director when making a provisional decision under paragraph 3 of Schedule 5 or paragraph 3 of Schedule 6.

**Guidance**

4. Rules may make provision as to-

    (a) the form and manner in which guidance is to be given;
    (b) the procedure to be followed if-
        (i) the Director takes further action with respect to an agreement after giving guidance that it is not likely to infringe the Chapter I prohibition; or

(ii) the Director takes further action with respect to conduct after giving guidance that it is not likely to infringe the Chapter II prohibition.

## Decisions

5.– (1) Rules may make provision as to-

(a) the form and manner in which notice of any decision is to be given;
(b) the person or persons to whom the notice is to be given;
(c) the manner in which the Director is to publish a decision;
(d) the procedure to be followed if-
    (i) the Director takes further action with respect to an agreement after having decided that it does not infringe the Chapter I prohibition; or
    (ii) the Director takes further action with respect to conduct after having decided that it does not infringe the Chapter II prohibition.

(2) In this paragraph "decision" means a decision of the Director (whether or not made on an application)-

(a) as to whether or not an agreement has infringed the Chapter I prohibition, or
(b) as to whether or not conduct has infringed the Chapter II prohibition,

and, in the case of an application for a decision under section 14 which includes a request for an individual exemption, includes a decision as to whether or not to grant the exemption.

## Individual exemptions

6. Rules may make provision as to-

(a) the procedure to be followed by the Director when deciding whether, in accordance with section 5-
    (i) to cancel an individual exemption that he has granted,
    (ii) to vary or remove any of its conditions or obligations, or
    (iii) to impose additional conditions or obligations;
(b) the form and manner in which notice of such a decision is to be given.

7. Rules may make provision as to-

(a) the form and manner in which an application under section 4(6) for the extension of an individual exemption is to be made;
(b) the circumstances in which the Director will consider such an application;
(c) the procedure to be followed by the Director when deciding whether to grant such an application;
(d) the form and manner in which notice of such a decision is to be given.

## Block exemptions

8. Rules may make provision as to-

(a) the form and manner in which notice of an agreement is to be given to the Director under subsection (1) of section 7;

(b) the procedure to be followed by the Director if he is acting under subsection (2) of that section;

(c) as to the procedure to be followed by the Director if he cancels a block exemption.

## Parallel exemptions

9.  Rules may make provision as to-

(a) the circumstances in which the Director may-
   (i) impose conditions or obligations in relation to a parallel exemption,
   (ii) vary or remove any such conditions or obligations,
   (iii) impose additional conditions or obligations, or
   (iv) cancel the exemption;

(b) as to the procedure to be followed by the Director if he is acting under section 10(5);

(c) the form and manner in which notice of a decision to take any of the steps in sub-paragraph (a) is to be given;

(d) the circumstances in which an exemption may be cancelled with retrospective effect.

## Section 11 exemptions

10. Rules may, with respect to any exemption provided by regulations made under section 11, make provision similar to that made with respect to parallel exemptions by section 10 or by rules under paragraph 9.

## Directions withdrawing exclusions

11. Rules may make provision as to the factors which the Director may take into account when he is determining the date on which a direction given under paragraph 4(1) of Schedule 1 or paragraph 2(3) or 9(3) of Schedule 3 is to have effect.

## Disclosure of information

12.- (1) Rules may make provision as to the circumstances in which the Director is to be required, before disclosing information given to him by a third party in connection with the exercise of any of the Director's functions under Part I, to give notice, and an opportunity to make representations, to the third party.

(2) In relation to the agreement (or conduct) concerned,

"third party" means a person who is not a party to the agreement (or who has not engaged in the conduct).

**Applications under section 47**

**13.** Rules may make provision as to-

(a) the period within which an application under section 47(1) must be made;

(b) the procedure to be followed by the Director in dealing with the application;

(c) the person or persons to whom notice of the Director's response to the application is to be given.

**Enforcement**

**14.** Rules may make provision as to the procedure to be followed when the Director takes action under any of sections 32 to 41 with respect to the enforcement of the provisions of this Part.

## SCHEDULE 10

### REGULATORS

### PART I

### MONOPOLIES

**1.** The amendments of the Fair Trading Act 1973 made by sections 66 and 67 of this Act are to have effect, not only in relation to the jurisdiction of the Director under the provisions amended, but also in relation to the jurisdiction under those provisions of each of the following-

(a) the Director General of Telecommunications;

(b) the Director General of Electricity Supply;

(c) the Director General of Electricity Supply for Northern Ireland;

(d) the Director General of Water Services;

(e) the Rail Regulator;

(f) the Director General of Gas Supply; and

(g) the Director General of Gas for Northern Ireland.

### PART II

### THE PROHIBITIONS

**Telecommunications**

**2.–** (1) In consequence of the repeal by this Act of provisions of the Competition Act 1980, the functions transferred by subsection (3) of section 50 of the Telecommunications Act 1984 (functions under 1973 and 1980 Acts) are no longer exercisable by the Director General of Telecommunications.

(2) Accordingly, that Act is amended as follows.

(3) In section 3 (general duties of Secretary of State and Director), in subsection (3)(b), for "section 50" substitute "section 50(1) or (2)".

(4) In section 3, after subsection (3A), insert-

"(3B) Subsections (1) and (2) above do not apply in relation to anything done by the Director in the exercise of functions assigned to him by section 50(3) below ("Competition Act functions").

(3C) The Director may nevertheless, when exercising any Competition Act function, have regard to any matter in respect of which a duty is imposed by subsection (1) or (2) above ("a general matter"), if it is a matter to which the Director General of Fair Trading could have regard when exercising that function; but that is not to be taken as implying that, in relation to any of the matters mentioned in subsection (3) or (3A) above, regard may not be had to any general matter."

(5) Section 50 is amended as follows.

(6) For subsection (3) substitute-

"(3) The Director shall be entitled to exercise, concurrently with the Director General of Fair Trading, the functions of that Director under the provisions of Part I of the Competition Act 1998 (other than sections 38(1) to (6) and 51), so far as relating to-

(a) agreements, decisions or concerted practices of the kind mentioned in section 2(1) of that Act, or
(b) conduct of the kind mentioned in section 18(1) of that Act,

which relate to commercial activities connected with telecommunications.

(3A) So far as necessary for the purposes of, or in connection with, the provisions of subsection (3) above, references in Part I of the Competition Act 1998 to the Director General of Fair Trading are to be read as including a reference to the Director (except in sections 38(1) to (6), 51, 52(6) and (8) and 54 of that Act and in any other provision of that Act where the context otherwise requires)."

(7) In subsection (4), omit paragraph (c) and the "and" immediately after it.

(8) In subsection (5), omit "or (3)".

(9) In subsection (6), for paragraph (b) substitute-

"(b) Part I of the Competition Act 1998 (other than sections 38(1) to (6) and 51),".

(10) In subsection (7), omit "or the 1980 Act".

**Gas**

3.– (1) In consequence of the repeal by this Act of provisions of the Competition Act 1980, the functions transferred by subsection (3) of section 36A of the Gas Act 1986 (functions with respect to competition) are no longer exercisable by the Director General of Gas Supply.

(2) Accordingly, that Act is amended as follows.

(3) In section 4 (general duties of Secretary of State and Director), after subsection (3), insert-

"(3A) Subsections (1) to (3) above and section 4A below do not apply in relation to anything done by the Director in the exercise of functions assigned to him by section 36A below ("Competition Act functions").

(3B) The Director may nevertheless, when exercising any Competition Act function, have regard to any matter in respect of which a duty is imposed by any of subsections (1) to (3) above or section 4A below, if it is a matter to which the Director General of Fair Trading could have regard when exercising that function."

(4) Section 36A is amended as follows.

(5) For subsection (3) substitute-

"(3) The Director shall be entitled to exercise, concurrently with the Director General of Fair Trading, the functions of that Director under the provisions of Part I of the Competition Act 1998 (other than sections 38(1) to (6) and 51), so far as relating to-

(a) agreements, decisions or concerted practices of the kind mentioned in section 2(1) of that Act, or
(b) conduct of the kind mentioned in section 18(1) of that Act,

which relate to the carrying on of activities to which this subsection applies.

(3A) So far as necessary for the purposes of, or in connection with, the provisions of subsection (3) above, references in Part I of the Competition Act 1998 to the Director General of Fair Trading are to be read as including a reference to the Director (except in sections 38(1) to (6), 51, 52(6) and (8) and 54 of that Act and in any other provision of that Act where the context otherwise requires)."

(6) In subsection (5)-

(a) for "transferred by", in each place, substitute "mentioned in";
(b) after paragraph (b), insert "and";
(c) omit paragraph (d) and the "and" immediately before it.

(7) In subsection (6), omit "or (3)".

(8) In subsection (7), for paragraph (b) substitute-

"(b) Part I of the Competition Act 1998 (other than sections 38(1) to (6) and 51),".

(9) In subsection (8)-

(a) omit "or under the 1980 Act";
(b) for "or (3) above" substitute "above and paragraph 1 of Schedule 10 to the Competition Act 1998".

(10) In subsection (9), omit "or the 1980 Act".

(11) In subsection (10), for the words from "transferred" to the end substitute "mentioned in subsection (2) or (3) above."

**Electricity**

**4.–** (1) In consequence of the repeal by this Act of provisions of the Competition Act 1980, the functions transferred by subsection (3) of section 43 of the Electricity Act 1989 (functions with respect to competition) are no longer exercisable by the Director General of Electricity Supply.

(2) Accordingly, that Act is amended as follows.

(3) In section 3 (general duties of Secretary of State and Director), after subsection (6), insert-

"(6A) Subsections (1) to (5) above do not apply in relation to anything done by the Director in the exercise of functions assigned to him by section 43(3) below ("Competition Act functions").

(6B) The Director may nevertheless, when exercising any Competition Act function, have regard to any matter in respect of which a duty is imposed by any of subsections (1) to (5) above ("a general matter"), if it is a matter to which the Director General of Fair Trading could have regard when exercising that function; but that is not to be taken as implying that, in the exercise of any function mentioned in subsection (6) above, regard may not be had to any general matter."

(4) Section 43 is amended as follows.

(5) For subsection (3) substitute-

"(3) The Director shall be entitled to exercise, concurrently with the Director General of Fair Trading, the functions of that Director under the provisions of Part I of the Competition Act 1998 (other than sections 38(1) to (6) and 51), so far as relating to-

(a) agreements, decisions or concerted practices of the kind mentioned in section 2(1) of that Act, or
(b) conduct of the kind mentioned in section 18(1) of that Act,

which relate to commercial activities connected with the generation, transmission or supply of electricity.

(3A) So far as necessary for the purposes of, or in connection with, the provisions of subsection (3) above, references in Part I of the Competition Act 1998 to the Director General of Fair Trading are to be read as including a reference to the Director (except in sections 38(1) to (6), 51, 52(6) and (8) and 54 of that Act and in any other provision of that Act where the context otherwise requires)."

(6) In subsection (4), omit paragraph (c) and the "and" immediately after it.

(7) In subsection (5), omit "or (3)".

(8) In subsection (6), for paragraph (b) substitute-

"(b) Part I of the Competition Act 1998 (other than sections 38(1) to (6) and 51),".

(9) In subsection (7), omit "or the 1980 Act".

**Water**

5.– (1) In consequence of the repeal by this Act of provisions of the Competition Act 1980, the functions exercisable by virtue of subsection (3) of section 31 of the Water Industry Act 1991 (functions of Director with respect to competition) are no longer exercisable by the Director General of Water Services.

(2) Accordingly, that Act is amended as follows.

(3) In section 2 (general duties with respect to water industry), in subsection (6)(a), at the beginning, insert "subject to subsection (6A) below".

(4) In section 2, after subsection (6), insert-

"(6A) Subsections (2) to (4) above do not apply in relation to anything done by the Director in the exercise of functions assigned to him by section 31(3) below ("Competition Act functions").

(6B) The Director may nevertheless, when exercising any Competition Act function, have regard to any matter in respect of which a duty is imposed by any of subsections (2) to (4) above, if it is a matter to which the Director General of Fair Trading could have regard when exercising that function."

(5) Section 31 is amended as follows.

(6) For subsection (3) substitute-

"(3) The Director shall be entitled to exercise, concurrently with the Director General of Fair Trading, the functions of that Director under the provisions of Part I of the Competition Act 1998 (other than sections 38(1) to (6) and 51), so far as relating to-

(a) agreements, decisions or concerted practices of the kind mentioned in section 2(1) of that Act, or
(b) conduct of the kind mentioned in section 18(1) of that Act,

which relate to commercial activities connected with the supply of water or securing a supply of water or with the provision or securing of sewerage services."

(7) In subsection (4)-

(a) for "to (3)" substitute "and (2)";
(b) omit paragraph (c) and the "and" immediately before it.

(8) After subsection (4), insert-

"(4A) So far as necessary for the purposes of, or in connection with, the provisions of subsection (3) above, references in Part I of the Competition Act 1998 to the Director General of Fair Trading are to be read as including a reference to the Director (except in sections 38(1) to (6), 51, 52(6) and (8) and 54 of that Act and in any other provision of that Act where the context otherwise requires)."

(9) In subsection (5), omit "or in subsection (3) above".

(10) In subsection (6), omit "or in subsection (3) above".

(11) In subsection (7), omit "or (3)".

(12) In subsection (8), for paragraph (b) substitute-

"(b) Part I of the Competition Act 1998 (other than sections 38(1) to (6) and 51),".

(13) In subsection (9), omit "or the 1980 Act".

## Railways

**6.**– (1) In consequence of the repeal by this Act of provisions of the Competition Act 1980, the functions transferred by subsection (3) of section 67 of the Railways Act 1993 (respective functions of the Regulator and the Director etc) are no longer exercisable by the Rail Regulator.

(2) Accordingly, that Act is amended as follows.

(3) In section 4 (general duties of the Secretary of State and the Regulator), after subsection (7), insert-

"(7A) Subsections (1) to (6) above do not apply in relation to anything done by the Regulator in the exercise of functions assigned to him by section 67(3) below ("Competition Act functions").

(7B) The Regulator may nevertheless, when exercising any Competition Act function, have regard to any matter in respect of which a duty is imposed by any of subsections (1) to (6) above, if it is a matter to which the Director General of Fair Trading could have regard when exercising that function."

(4) Section 67 is amended as follows.

(5) For subsection (3) substitute-

"(3) The Regulator shall be entitled to exercise, concurrently with the Director, the functions of the Director under the provisions of Part I of the Competition Act 1998 (other than sections 38(1) to (6) and 51), so far as relating to-

(a) agreements, decisions or concerted practices of the kind mentioned in section 2(1) of that Act, or
(b) conduct of the kind mentioned in section 18(1) of that Act,

which relate to the supply of railway services.

(3A) So far as necessary for the purposes of, or in connection with, the provisions of subsection (3) above, references in Part I of the Competition Act 1998 to the Director are to be read as including a reference to the Regulator (except in sections 38(1) to (6), 51, 52(6) and (8) and 54 of that Act and in any other provision of that Act where the context otherwise requires)."

(6) In subsection (4), omit paragraph (c) and the "and" immediately after it.

(7) In subsection (6)(a), omit "or (3)".

(8) In subsection (8), for paragraph (b) substitute-

"(b) Part I of the Competition Act 1998 (other than sections 38(1) to (6) and 51),".

(9) In subsection (9)-

(a) omit "or under the 1980 Act";
(b) for "or (3) above" substitute "above and paragraph 1 of Schedule 10 to the Competition Act 1998".

## Part III

### The Prohibitions: Northern Ireland

**Electricity**

7.– (1) In consequence of the repeal by this Act of provisions of the Competition Act 1980, the functions transferred by paragraph (3) of Article 46 of the Electricity (Northern Ireland) Order 1992 (functions with respect to competition) are no longer exercisable by the Director General of Electricity Supply for Northern Ireland.

(2) Accordingly, that Order is amended as follows.

(3) In Article 6 (general duties of the Director), after paragraph (2), add-

"(3) Paragraph (1) does not apply in relation to anything done by the Director in the exercise of functions assigned to him by Article 46(3) ("Competition Act functions").

(4) The Director may nevertheless, when exercising any Competition Act function, have regard to any matter in respect of which a duty is imposed by paragraph (1) ("a general matter"), if it is a matter to which the Director General of Fair Trading could have regard when exercising that function; but that is not to be taken as implying that, in the exercise of any function mentioned in Article 4(7) or paragraph (2), regard may not be had to any general matter."

(4) Article 46 is amended as follows.

(5) For paragraph (3) substitute-

"(3) The Director shall be entitled to exercise, concurrently with the Director General of Fair Trading, the functions of that Director under the provisions of Part I of the Competition Act 1998 (other than sections 38(1) to (6) and 51), so far as relating to-

(a) agreements, decisions or concerted practices of the kind mentioned in section 2(1) of that Act, or

(b) conduct of the kind mentioned in section 18(1) of that Act,

which relate to commercial activities connected with the generation, transmission or supply of electricity.

(3A) So far as necessary for the purposes of, or in connection with, the provisions of paragraph (3), references in Part I of the Competition Act 1998 to the Director General of Fair Trading are to be read as including a reference to the Director (except in sections 38(1) to (6), 51, 52(6) and (8) and 54 of that Act and in any other provision of that Act where the context otherwise requires)."

(6) In paragraph (4), omit sub-paragraph (c) and the "and" immediately after it.

(7) In paragraph (5), omit "or (3)".

(8) In paragraph (6), for sub-paragraph (b) substitute-

"(b) Part I of the Competition Act 1998 (other than sections 38(1) to (6) and 51),".

(9) In paragraph (7), omit "or the 1980 Act".

## Gas

8.– (1) In consequence of the repeal by this Act of provisions of the Competition Act 1980, the functions transferred by paragraph (3) of Article 23 of the Gas (Northern Ireland) Order 1996 (functions with respect to competition) are no longer exercisable by the Director General of Gas for Northern Ireland.

(2) Accordingly, that Order is amended as follows.

(3) In Article 5 (general duties of the Department and Director), after paragraph (4), insert-

"(4A) Paragraphs (2) to (4) do not apply in relation to anything done by the Director in the exercise of functions assigned to him by Article 23(3) ("Competition Act functions").

(4B) The Director may nevertheless, when exercising any Competition Act function, have regard to any matter in respect of which a duty is imposed by any of paragraphs (2) to (4), if it is a matter to which the Director General of Fair Trading could have regard when exercising that function."

(4) Article 23 is amended as follows.

(5) For paragraph (3) substitute-

"(3) The Director shall be entitled to exercise, concurrently with the Director General of Fair Trading, the functions of that Director under the provisions of Part I of the Competition Act 1998 (other than sections 38(1) to (6) and 51), so far as relating to-

(a) agreements, decisions or concerted practices of the kind mentioned in section 2(1) of that Act, or

(b) conduct of the kind mentioned in section 18(1) of that Act,

connected with the conveyance, storage or supply of gas.

(3A) So far as necessary for the purposes of, or in connection with, the provisions of paragraph (3), references in Part I of the Competition Act 1998 to the Director General of Fair Trading are to be read as including a reference to the Director (except in sections 38(1) to (6), 51, 52(6) and (8) and 54 of that Act and in any other provision of that Act where the context otherwise requires)."

(6) In paragraph (4)-

(a) for "transferred by", in each place, substitute "mentioned in";
(b) after sub-paragraph (b), insert "and";
(c) omit sub-paragraph (d) and the "and" immediately before it.

(7) In paragraph (5), omit "or (3)".

(8) In paragraph (6), for sub-paragraph (b) substitute-

"(b) Part I of the Competition Act 1998 (other than sections 38(1) to (6) and 51),".

(9) In paragraph (7)-

(a) omit "or under the 1980 Act";
(b) for "or (3)" substitute "and paragraph 1 of Schedule 10 to the Competition Act 1998".

(10) In paragraph (8), omit "or the 1980 Act".

(11) In paragraph (9), for the words from "transferred" to the end substitute "mentioned in paragraph (2) or (3)."

PART IV

UTILITIES: MINOR AND CONSEQUENTIAL AMENDMENTS

**The Telecommunications Act 1984 (c.12)**

**9.**– (1) The Telecommunications Act 1984 is amended as follows.

(2) In section 13 (licence modification references to Competition Commission), for subsections (9) and (10) substitute-

"(9) The provisions mentioned in subsection (9A) are to apply in relation to references under this section as if-

(a) the functions of the Competition Commission in relation to those references were functions under the Fair Trading Act 1973 (in this Act referred to as "the 1973 Act");

(b) the expression "merger reference" included a reference under this section;

(c) in section 70 of the 1973 Act-

(i) references to the Secretary of State were references to the Director, and

(ii) the reference to three months were a reference to six months.

(9A) The provisions are-

(a) sections 70 (time limit for report on merger) and 85 (attendance of witnesses and production of documents) of the 1973 Act;

(b) Part II of Schedule 7 to the Competition Act 1998 (performance of the Competition Commission's general functions); and

(c) section 24 of the Competition Act 1980 (modification of provisions about performance of such functions).

(10) For the purposes of references under this section, the Secretary of State is to appoint not less than three members of the Competition Commission.

(10A) In selecting a group to perform the Commission's functions in relation to any such reference, the chairman of the Commission must select up to three of the members appointed under subsection (10) to be members of the group."

(3) In section 14, omit subsection (2) (which falls with the repeal of the Restrictive Trade Practices Act 1976).

(4) In section 16 (securing compliance with licence conditions), in subsection (5), after paragraph (a), omit "or" and after paragraph (b), insert "or

(c) that the most appropriate way of proceeding is under the Competition Act 1998."

(5) In section 50 (functions under 1973 and 1980 Acts), after subsection (6), insert-

"(6A) Section 93B of the 1973 Act (offences of supplying false or misleading information) is to have effect so far as relating to functions exercisable by the Director by virtue of-

(a) subsection (2) above and paragraph 1 of Schedule 10 to the Competition Act 1998, or

(b) paragraph 1 of Schedule 2 to the Deregulation and Contracting Out Act 1994,

as if the reference in section 93B(1)(a) to the Director General of Fair Trading included a reference to the Director."

(6) In section 95 (modification by orders under other enactments)-

(a) in subsection (1), omit "or section 10(2)(a) of the 1980 Act";

(b) in subsection (2)-

(i) after paragraph (a), insert "or";

(ii) omit paragraph (c) and the "or" immediately before it;

(c) in subsection (3), omit "or the 1980 Act".

(7) In section 101(3) (general restrictions on disclosure of information)-

    (a) omit paragraphs (d) and (e) (which refer to the Restrictive Trade Practices Act 1976 and the Resale Prices Act 1976);

    (b) after paragraph (m), insert-

"(n) the Competition Act 1998".

(8) At the end of section 101, insert-

"(6) Information obtained by the Director in the exercise of functions which are exercisable concurrently with the Director General of Fair Trading under Part I of the Competition Act 1998 is subject to sections 55 and 56 of that Act (disclosure) and not to subsections (1) to (5) of this section."

### The Gas Act 1986 (c.44)

10.– (1) The Gas Act 1986 is amended as follows.

(2) In section 24 (modification references to the Competition Commission), for subsection (7) substitute-

"(7) The provisions mentioned in subsection (7A) are to apply in relation to references under this section as if-

    (a) the functions of the Competition Commission in relation to those references were functions under the Fair Trading Act 1973;

    (b) the expression "merger reference" included a reference under this section;

    (c) in section 70 of the Fair Trading Act 1973-

        (i)  references to the Secretary of State were references to the Director, and

        (ii) the reference to three months were a reference to six months.

(7A) The provisions are-

    (a) sections 70 (time limit for report on merger) and 85 (attendance of witnesses and production of documents) of the Fair Trading Act 1973;

    (b) Part II of Schedule 7 to the Competition Act 1998 (performance of the Competition Commission's general functions); and

    (c) section 24 of the Competition Act 1980 (modification of provisions about performance of such functions)."

(3) In section 25, omit subsection (2) (which falls with the repeal of the Restrictive Trade Practices Act 1976).

(4) In section 27 (modification by order under other enactments)-

    (a) in subsection (1), omit "or section 10(2)(a) of the Competition Act 1980";

    (b) in subsection (3)(a), omit from "or" to "competition reference";

    (c) in subsection (6), omit "or the said Act of 1980".

(5) In section 28 (orders for securing compliance with certain provisions), in subsection (5), after paragraph (aa), omit "or" and after paragraph (b), insert "or

(c) that the most appropriate way of proceeding is under the Competition Act 1998."

(6) In section 42(3) (general restrictions on disclosure of information)-

(a) omit paragraphs (e) and (f) (which refer to the Restrictive Trade Practices Act 1976 and the Resale Prices Act 1976);
(b) after paragraph (n), insert-

"(o) the Competition Act 1998".

(7) At the end of section 42, insert-

"(7) Information obtained by the Director in the exercise of functions which are exercisable concurrently with the Director General of Fair Trading under Part I of the Competition Act 1998 is subject to sections 55 and 56 of that Act (disclosure) and not to subsections (1) to (6) of this section."

## The Water Act 1989 (c.15)

**11.** In section 174(3) of the Water Act 1989 (general restrictions on disclosure of information)-

(a) omit paragraphs (d) and (e) (which refer to the Restrictive Trade Practices Act 1976 and the Resale Prices Act 1976);
(b) after paragraph (l), insert-

"(ll) the Competition Act 1998".

## The Electricity Act 1989 (c.29)

**12.–** (1) The Electricity Act 1989 is amended as follows.

(2) In section 12 (modification references to Competition Commission), for subsections (8) and (9) substitute-

"(8) The provisions mentioned in subsection (8A) are to apply in relation to references under this section as if-

(a) the functions of the Competition Commission in relation to those references were functions under the 1973 Act;
(b) the expression "merger reference" included a reference under this section;
(c) in section 70 of the 1973 Act-
    (i)  references to the Secretary of State were references to the Director, and
    (ii) the reference to three months were a reference to six months.

(8A) The provisions are-

(a) sections 70 (time limit for report on merger) and 85 (attendance of witnesses and production of documents) of the 1973 Act;

   (b) Part II of Schedule 7 to the Competition Act 1998 (performance of the Competition Commission's general functions); and

   (c) section 24 of the 1980 Act (modification of provisions about performance of such functions).

(9) For the purposes of references under this section, the Secretary of State is to appoint not less than eight members of the Competition Commission.

(9A) In selecting a group to perform the Commission's functions in relation to any such reference, the chairman of the Commission must select up to three of the members appointed under subsection (9) to be members of the group."

(3) In section 13, omit subsection (2) (which falls with the repeal of the Restrictive Trade Practices Act 1976).

(4) In section 15 (modification by order under other enactments)-

   (a) in subsection (1), omit paragraph (b) and the "or" immediately before it;
   (b) in subsection (2)-
      (i) after paragraph (a), insert "or";
      (ii) omit paragraph (c) and the "or" immediately before it;
   (c) in subsection (3), omit "or the 1980 Act".

(5) In section 25 (orders for securing compliance), in subsection (5), after paragraph (b), omit "or" and after paragraph (c), insert "or

   (d) that the most appropriate way of proceeding is under the Competition Act 1998."

(6) In section 43 (functions with respect to competition), after subsection (6), insert-

"(6A) Section 93B of the 1973 Act (offences of supplying false or misleading information) is to have effect so far as relating to functions exercisable by the Director by virtue of-

   (a) subsection (2) above and paragraph 1 of Schedule 10 to the Competition Act 1998, or
   (b) paragraph 4 of Schedule 2 to the Deregulation and Contracting Out Act 1994,

as if the reference in section 93B(1)(a) to the Director General of Fair Trading included a reference to the Director."

(7) In section 57(3) (general restrictions on disclosure of information)-

   (a) omit paragraphs (d) and (e) (which refer to the Restrictive Trade Practices Act 1976 and the Resale Prices Act 1976);
   (b) after paragraph (no), insert-

"(nop) the Competition Act 1998".

(8) At the end of section 57, insert-

"(7) Information obtained by the Director in the exercise of functions which are exercisable concurrently with the Director General of Fair Trading under Part I of the Competition Act 1998 is subject to sections 55 and 56 of that Act (disclosure) and not to subsections (1) to (6) of this section."

**The Water Industry Act 1991 (c.56)**

13.– (1) The Water Industry Act 1991 is amended as follows.

(2) In section 12(5) (determinations under conditions of appointment)-

(a) after "this Act", insert "or";
(b) omit "or the 1980 Act".

(3) In section 14 (modification references to Competition Commission), for subsections (7) and (8) substitute-

"(7) The provisions mentioned in subsection (7A) are to apply in relation to references under this section as if-

(a) the functions of the Competition Commission in relation to those references were functions under the 1973 Act;
(b) the expression "merger reference" included a reference under this section;
(c) in section 70 of the 1973 Act-
    (i) references to the Secretary of State were references to the Director, and
    (ii) the reference to three months were a reference to six months.

(7A) The provisions are-

(a) sections 70 (time limit for report on merger) and 85 (attendance of witnesses and production of documents) of the 1973 Act;
(b) Part II of Schedule 7 to the Competition Act 1998 (performance of the Competition Commission's general functions); and
(c) section 24 of the 1980 Act (modification of provisions about performance of such functions).

(8) For the purposes of references under this section, the Secretary of State is to appoint not less than eight members of the Competition Commission.

(8A) In selecting a group to perform the Commission's functions in relation to any such reference, the chairman of the Commission must select one or more of the members appointed under subsection (8) to be members of the group."

(4) In section 15, omit subsection (2) (which falls with the repeal of the Restrictive Trade Practices Act 1976).

(5) In section 17 (modification by order under other enactments)-

(a) in subsection (1), omit paragraph (b) and the "or" immediately before it;
(b) in subsection (2)-
    (i) after paragraph (a), insert "or";
    (ii) omit paragraph (c) and the "or" immediately before it;

(c) in subsection (4), omit "or the 1980 Act".

(6) In section 19 (exceptions to duty to enforce), after subsection (1), insert-

"(1A) The Director shall not be required to make an enforcement order, or to confirm a provisional enforcement order, if he is satisfied that the most appropriate way of proceeding is under the Competition Act 1998."

(7) In section 19(3), after "subsection (1) above", insert "or, in the case of the Director, is satisfied as mentioned in subsection (1A) above,".

(8) In section 31 (functions of Director with respect to competition), after subsection (8), insert-

"(8A) Section 93B of the 1973 Act (offences of supplying false or misleading information) is to have effect so far as relating to functions exercisable by the Director by virtue of-

(a) subsection (2) above and paragraph 1 of Schedule 10 to the Competition Act 1998, or
(b) paragraph 8 of Schedule 2 to the Deregulation and Contracting Out Act 1994,

as if the reference in section 93B(1)(a) to the Director General of Fair Trading included a reference to the Director."

(9) After section 206(9) (restriction on disclosure of information), insert-

"(9A) Information obtained by the Director in the exercise of functions which are exercisable concurrently with the Director General of Fair Trading under Part I of the Competition Act 1998 is subject to sections 55 and 56 of that Act (disclosure) and not to subsections (1) to (9) of this section."

(10) In Schedule 15 (disclosure of information), in Part II (enactments in respect of which disclosure may be made)-

(a) omit the entries relating to the Restrictive Trade Practices Act 1976 and the Resale Prices Act 1976;
(b) after the entry relating to the Railways Act 1993, insert the entry-

"The Competition Act 1998".

### The Water Resources Act 1991 (c.57)

14. In Schedule 24 to the Water Resources Act 1991 (disclosure of information), in Part II (enactments in respect of which disclosure may be made)-

(a) omit the entries relating to the Restrictive Trade Practices Act 1976 and the Resale Prices Act 1976;
(b) after the entry relating to the Coal Industry Act 1994, insert the entry-

"The Competition Act 1998".

**The Railways Act 1993 (c.43)**

15.– (1) The Railways Act 1993 is amended as follows.

(2) In section 13 (modification references to the Competition Commission), for subsection (8) substitute-

"(8) The provisions mentioned in subsection (8A) are to apply in relation to references under this section as if-

(a) the functions of the Competition Commission in relation to those references were functions under the 1973 Act;
(b) the expression "merger reference" included a reference under this section;
(c) in section 70 of the 1973 Act-
(i) references to the Secretary of State were references to the Director, and
(ii) the reference to three months were a reference to six months.

(8A) The provisions are-

(a) sections 70 (time limit for report on merger) and 85 (attendance of witnesses and production of documents) of the 1973 Act;
(b) Part II of Schedule 7 to the Competition Act 1998 (performance of the Competition Commission's general functions); and
(c) section 24 of the Competition Act 1980 (in this Part referred to as "the 1980 Act") (modification of provisions about performance of such functions)."

(3) In section 14, omit subsection (2) (which falls with the repeal of the Restrictive Trade Practices Act 1976).

(4) In section 16 (modification by order under other enactments)-

(a) in subsection (1), omit paragraph (b) and the "or" immediately before it;
(b) in subsection (2)-
(i) after paragraph (a), insert "or";
(ii) omit paragraph (c) and the "or" immediately before it;
(c) in subsection (5), omit "or the 1980 Act".

(5) In section 22, after subsection (6), insert-

"(6A) Neither the Director General of Fair Trading nor the Regulator may exercise, in respect of an access agreement, the powers given by section 32 (enforcement directions) or section 35(2) (interim directions) of the Competition Act 1998.

(6B) Subsection (6A) does not apply to the exercise of the powers given by section 35(2) in respect of conduct-

(a) which is connected with an access agreement; and
(b) in respect of which section 35(1)(b) of that Act applies."

(6) In section 55 (orders for securing compliance), after subsection (5), insert-

"(5A) The Regulator shall not make a final order, or make or confirm a provisional order, in relation to a licence holder or person under closure restrictions if he is satisfied that the most appropriate way of proceeding is under the Competition Act 1998."

(7) In section 55-

(a) in subsection (6), after "subsection (5)", insert "or (5A)";
(b) in subsection (11), for "subsection (10)" substitute "subsections (5A) and (10)".

(8) Omit section 131 (modification of Restrictive Trade Practices Act 1976).

(9) In section 145(3) (general restrictions on disclosure of information)-

(a) omit paragraphs (d) and (e) (which refer to the Restrictive Trade Practices Act 1976 and the Resale Prices Act 1976);
(b) after paragraph (q), insert-

"(qq) the Competition Act 1998."

(10) After section 145(6), insert-

"(6A) Information obtained by the Regulator in the exercise of functions which are exercisable concurrently with the Director General of Fair Trading under Part I of the Competition Act 1998 is subject to sections 55 and 56 of that Act (disclosure) and not to subsections (1) to (6) of this section."

### The Channel Tunnel Rail Link Act 1996 (c.61)

16.– (1) The Channel Tunnel Rail Link Act 1996 is amended as follows.

(2) In section 21 (duties as to exercise of regulatory functions), in subsection (6), at the end of the paragraph about regulatory functions, insert "other than any functions assigned to him by virtue of section 67(3) of that Act ("Competition Act functions").

(7) The Regulator may, when exercising any Competition Act function, have regard to any matter to which he would have regard if-

(a) he were under the duty imposed by subsection (1) or (2) above in relation to that function; and
(b) the matter is one to which the Director General of Fair Trading could have regard if he were exercising that function."

(3) In section 22 (restriction of functions in relation to competition etc.), for subsection (3) substitute-

"(3) The Rail Regulator shall not be entitled to exercise any functions assigned to him by section 67(3) of the Railways Act 1993 (by virtue of which he exercises concurrently with the Director General of Fair Trading certain functions under Part I of the Competition Act 1998 so far as relating to matters connected with the supply of railway services) in relation to-

    (a) any agreements, decisions or concerted practices of the kind mentioned in
section 2(1) of that Act that have been entered into or taken by, or

    (b) any conduct of the kind mentioned in section 18(1) of that Act that has been
engaged in by,

a rail link undertaker in connection with the supply of railway services, so far as
relating to the rail link."

PART V

MINOR AND CONSEQUENTIAL AMENDMENTS: NORTHERN IRELAND

## The Electricity (Northern Ireland) Order 1992

**17.**– (1) The Electricity (Northern Ireland) Order 1992 is amended as follows.

(2) In Article 15 (modification references to Competition Commission), for paragraphs
(8) and (9) substitute-

"(8) The provisions mentioned in paragraph (8A) are to apply in relation to references
under this Article as if-

    (a) the functions of the Competition Commission in relation to those references
were functions under the 1973 Act;

    (b) "merger reference" included a reference under this Article;

    (c) in section 70 of the 1973 Act-

        (i) references to the Secretary of State were references to the Director, and

        (ii) the reference to three months were a reference to six months.

(8A) The provisions are-

    (a) sections 70 (time limit for report on merger) and 85 (attendance of witnesses
and production of documents) of the 1973 Act;

    (b) Part II of Schedule 7 to the Competition Act 1998 (performance of the
Competition Commission's general functions); and

    (c) section 24 of the 1980 Act (modification of provisions about performance of
such functions).

(9) The Secretary of State may appoint members of the Competition Commission for
the purposes of references under this Article.

(9A) In selecting a group to perform the Commission's functions in relation to any
such reference, the chairman of the Commission must select up to three of the
members appointed under paragraph (9) to be members of the group."

(3) In Article 16, omit paragraph (2) (which falls with the repeal of the Restrictive
Trade Practices Act 1976).

(4) In Article 18 (modification by order under other statutory provisions)-

    (a) in paragraph (1), omit sub-paragraph (b) and the "or" immediately before it;

    (b) in paragraph (2)-

(i) after sub-paragraph (a), insert "or";

(ii) omit sub-paragraph (c) and the "or" immediately before it;

(c) in paragraph (3), omit "or the 1980 Act".

(5) In Article 28 (orders for securing compliance), in paragraph (5), after sub-paragraph (b), omit "or" and after sub-paragraph (c), insert "or

(d) that the most appropriate way of proceeding is under the Competition Act 1998."

(6) In Article 46 (functions with respect to competition), after paragraph (6), insert-

"(6A) Section 93B of the 1973 Act (offences of supplying false or misleading information) is to have effect so far as relating to functions exercisable by the Director by virtue of-

(a) paragraph (2) and paragraph 1 of Schedule 10 to the Competition Act 1998, or

(b) paragraph 5 of Schedule 2 to the Deregulation and Contracting Out Act 1994,

as if the reference in section 93B(l)(a) to the Director General of Fair Trading included a reference to the Director."

(7) In Article 61(3) (general restrictions on disclosure of information)-

(a) omit sub-paragraphs (f) and (g) (which refer to the Restrictive Trade Practices Act 1976 and the Resale Prices Act 1976);

(b) after sub-paragraph (t), add-

"(u) the Competition Act 1998".

(8) At the end of Article 61, insert-

"(7) Information obtained by the Director in the exercise of functions which are exercisable concurrently with the Director General of Fair Trading under Part I of the Competition Act 1998 is subject to sections 55 and 56 of that Act (disclosure) and not to paragraphs (1) to (6)."

(9) In Schedule 12, omit paragraph 16 (which amends the Restrictive Trade Practices Act 1976).

**The Gas (Northern Ireland) Order 1996**

**18.**– (1) The Gas (Northern Ireland) Order 1996 is amended as follows.

(2) In Article 15 (modification references to the Competition Commission), for paragraph (9) substitute-

"(9) The provisions mentioned in paragraph (9A) are to apply in relation to references under this Article as if-

(a) the functions of the Competition Commission in relation to those references were functions under the 1973 Act;

(b) "merger reference" included a reference under this Article;

(c) in section 70 of the 1973 Act-
    (i)  references to the Secretary of State were references to the Director, and
    (ii) the reference to three months were a reference to six months.

(9A) The provisions are-

    (a) sections 70 (time limit for report on merger) and 85 (attendance of witnesses and production of documents) of the 1973 Act;
    (b) Part II of Schedule 7 to the Competition Act 1998 (performance of the Competition Commission's general functions); and
    (c) section 24 of the 1980 Act (modification of provisions about performance of such functions)."

(3) In Article 16, omit paragraph (2) (which falls with the repeal of the Restrictive Trade Practices Act 1976).

(4) In Article 18 (modification by order under other statutory provisions)-

    (a) in paragraph (1), omit sub-paragraph (b) and the "or" immediately before it;
    (b) in paragraph (3)-
        (i)  after sub-paragraph (a), insert "or";
        (ii) omit sub-paragraph (c) and the "or" immediately before it;
    (c) in paragraph (5), omit "or the 1980 Act".

(5) In Article 19 (orders for securing compliance), in paragraph (5), after sub-paragraph (b), omit "or" and after sub-paragraph (c), insert "or

    (d) that the most appropriate way of proceeding is under the Competition Act 1998."

(6) In Article 44(4) (general restrictions on disclosure of information)-

    (a) omit sub-paragraphs (f) and (g) (which refer to the Restrictive Trade Practices Act 1976 and the Resale Prices Act 1976);
    (b) after sub-paragraph (u), add-

"(v) the Competition Act 1998".

(7) At the end of Article 44, insert-

"(8) Information obtained by the Director in the exercise of functions which are exercisable concurrently with the Director General of Fair Trading under Part I of the Competition Act 1998 is subject to sections 55 and 56 of that Act (disclosure) and not to paragraphs (1) to (7)."

## SCHEDULE 11

INTERPRETATION OF SECTION 55

**Relevant functions**

1.  In section 55(3) "relevant functions" means any function under-

    (a)  Part I or any enactment repealed in consequence of Part I;
    (b)  the Fair Trading Act 1973 (c. 41) or the Competition Act 1980 (c. 21);
    (c)  the Estate Agents Act 1979 (c. 38);
    (d)  the Telecommunications Act 1984 (c. 12);
    (e)  the Gas Act 1986 (c. 44) or the Gas Act 1995 (c. 45);
    (f)  the Gas (Northern Ireland) Order 1996;
    (g)  the Airports Act 1986 (c. 31) or Part IV of the Airports (Northern Ireland) Order 1994;
    (h)  the Financial Services Act 1986 (c. 60);
    (i)  the Electricity Act 1989 (c. 29) or the Electricity (Northern Ireland) Order 1992;
    (j)  the Broadcasting Act 1990 (c. 42) or the Broadcasting Act 1996 (c. 55);
    (k)  the Courts and Legal Services Act 1990 (c. 41);
    (l)  the Water Industry Act 1991 (c. 56), the Water Resources Act 1991 (c. 57), the Statutory Water Companies Act 1991 (c. 58), the Land Drainage Act 1991 (c. 59) and the Water Consolidation (Consequential Provisions) Act 1991 (c. 60);
    (m) the Railways Act 1993 (c. 43);
    (n)  the Coal Industry Act 1994 (c. 21);
    (o)  the EC Competition Law (Articles 88 and 89) Enforcement Regulations 1996;
    (p)  any subordinate legislation made (whether before or after the passing of this Act) for the purpose of implementing Council Directive No. 91/440/EEC of 29th July 1991 on the development of the Community's railways, Council Directive No. 95/18/EC of 19th June 1995 on the licensing of railway undertakings or Council Directive No. 95/19/EC of 19th June 1995 on the allocation of railway infrastructure capacity and the charging of infrastructure fees.

**Designated persons**

2.  In section 55(3) "designated person" means any of the following-

    (a)  the Director;
    (b)  the Director General of Telecommunications;
    (c)  the Independent Television Commission;
    (d)  the Director General of Gas Supply;
    (e)  the Director General of Gas for Northern Ireland;
    (f)  the Civil Aviation Authority;
    (g)  the Director General of Water Services;
    (h)  the Director General of Electricity Supply;
    (i)  the Director General of Electricity Supply for Northern Ireland;
    (j)  the Rail Regulator;

(k) the Director of Passenger Rail Franchising;

(l) the International Rail Regulator;

(m) the Authorised Conveyancing Practitioners Board;

(n) the Scottish Conveyancing and Executry Services Board;

(o) the Coal Authority;

(p) the Monopolies and Mergers Commission;

(q) the Competition Commission;

(r) the Securities and Investments Board;

(s) any Minister of the Crown or any Northern Ireland department.


# SCHEDULE 12

## MINOR AND CONSEQUENTIAL AMENDMENTS

### The Fair Trading Act 1973 (c.41)

**1.**– (1) The Fair Trading Act 1973 is amended as follows.

(2) Omit section 4 and Schedule 3 (which make provision in respect of the Monopolies and Mergers Commission).

(3) Omit-

(a) section 10(2),

(b) section 54(5),

(c) section 78(3),

(d) paragraph 3(1) and (2) of Schedule 8,

(which fall with the repeal of the Restrictive Trade Practices Act 1976).

(4) In section 10 (supplementary provisions about monopoly situations), in subsection (8), for "to (7)" substitute "and (3) to (7)".

(5) In sections 35 and 37 to 41, for "the Restrictive Practices Court", in each place, substitute "a relevant Court".

(6) After section 41, insert-

"Meaning of "relevant Court".

41A. In this Part of this Act, "relevant Court", in relation to proceedings in respect of a course of conduct maintained in the course of a business, means any of the following courts in whose jurisdiction that business is carried on-

(a) in England and Wales or Northern Ireland, the High Court;

(b) in Scotland, the Court of Session."

(7) In section 42 (appeals from decisions or orders of courts under Part III)-

(a) in subsection (1), at the end, add "; but this subsection is subject to subsection (3) of this section";

(b) in subsection (2)(b), after "Scotland," insert "from the sheriff court"; and

(c) after subsection (2), add-

"(3) A decision or order of the Court of Session as the relevant Court may be reviewed, whether on a question of fact or on a question of law, by reclaiming to the Inner House."

(8) Omit section 45 (power of the Director to require information about complex monopoly situations).

(9) In section 81 (procedure in carrying out investigations)-

    (a) in subsection (1)-
        (i) in the words before paragraph (a), omit from "and the Commission" to "of this Act)";
        (ii) in paragraph (b), omit "or the Commission, as the case may be," and "or of the Commission";
    (b) in subsection (2), omit "or the Commission" and "or of the Commission"; and
    (c) in subsection (3), omit from "and, in the case," to "85 of this Act" and "or the Commission, as the case may be,".

(10) In section 85 (attendance of witnesses and production of documents on investigations by Competition Commission of references under the Fair Trading Act 1973), in subsection (1)(b)-

    (a) after "purpose", insert "(i)";
    (b) after the second "notice", insert "or
        (ii) any document which falls within a category of document which is specified, or described, in the notice,".

(11) In section 85, in subsection (1)(c), after "estimates" (in both places), insert "forecasts".

(12) In section 85, after subsection (1), insert-

"(1A) For the purposes of subsection (1) above-

    (a) "document" includes information recorded in any form;
    (b) the power to require the production of documents includes power to take copies of, or extracts from, any document produced; and
    (c) in relation to information recorded otherwise than in legible form, the power to require it to be produced includes power to require it to be produced in legible form, so far as the means to do so are within the custody or under the control of the person on whom the requirement is imposed."

(13) In section 85(2), for "any such investigation" substitute "an investigation of the kind mentioned in subsection (1)".

(14) In section 133 (general restrictions on disclosure of information), in subsection (2)(a), after "the Coal Industry Act 1994" insert "or the Competition Act 1998".

(15) In section 135(1) (financial provisions)-

(a) in the words before paragraph (a) and in paragraph (b), omit "or the Commission"; and

(b) omit paragraph (a).

### The Energy Act 1976 (c.76)

2. In the Energy Act 1976, omit section 5 (temporary relief from restrictive practices law in relation to certain agreements connected with petroleum).

### The Estate Agents Act 1979 (c.38)

3. In section 10(3) of the Estate Agents Act 1979 (restriction on disclosure of information), in paragraph (a)-

(a) omit "or the Restrictive Trade Practices Act 1976"; and

(b) after "the Coal Industry Act 1994", insert "or the Competition Act 1998".

### The Competition Act 1980 (c.21)

4.– (1) The Competition Act 1980 is amended as follows.

(2) In section 11(8) (public bodies and other persons referred to the Commission), omit paragraph (b) and the "and" immediately before it.

(3) For section 11(9) (which makes provision for certain functions of the Competition Commission under the Fair Trading Act 1973 to apply in relation to references under the Competition Act 1980) substitute-

"(9) The provisions mentioned in subsection (9A) are to apply in relation to a reference under this section as if-

(a) the functions of the Competition Commission under this section were functions under the Fair Trading Act 1973;

(b) the expression "merger reference" included a reference to the Commission under this section; and

(c) in paragraph 20(2)(a) of Schedule 7 to the Competition Act 1998, the reference to section 56 of the Fair Trading Act 1973 were a reference to section 12 below.

(9A) The provisions are-

(a) sections 70 (time limit for report on merger), 84 (public interest) and 85 (attendance of witnesses and production of documents) of the Fair Trading Act 1973; and

(b) Part II of Schedule 7 to the Competition Act 1998 (performance of the Competition Commission's general functions)."

(4) In section 13 (investigation of prices directed by Secretary of State)-

(a) in subsection (1), omit from "but the giving" to the end;

(b) for subsection (6) substitute-

"(6) For the purposes of an investigation under this section the Director may, by notice in writing signed by him-

(a) require any person to produce-
    (i)  at a time and a place specified in the notice,
    (ii) to the Director or to any person appointed by him for the purpose,

any documents which are specified or described in the notice and which are documents in his custody or under his control and relating to any matter relevant to the investigation; or

(b) require any person carrying on any business to-
    (i)  furnish to the Director such estimates, forecasts, returns or other information as may be specified or described in the notice; and
    (ii) specify the time, manner and form in which any such estimates, forecasts, returns or information are to be furnished.

(7) No person shall be compelled, for the purpose of any investigation under this section-

(a) to produce any document which he could not be compelled to produce in civil proceedings before the High Court or, in Scotland, the Court of Session; or
(b) in complying with any requirement for the furnishing of information, to give any information which he could not be compelled to give in evidence in such proceedings.

(8) Subsections (6) to (8) of section 85 of the Fair Trading Act 1973 (enforcement provisions relating to notices requiring production of documents etc.) shall apply in relation to a notice under subsection (6) above as they apply in relation to a notice under section 85(1) but as if, in section 85(7), for the words from "any one" to "the Commission" there were substituted "the Director.""

(5) In section 15 (special provisions for agricultural schemes) omit subsections (2)(b), (3) and (4).

(6) In section 16 (reports), omit subsection (3).

(7) In section 17 (publication etc. of reports)-

(a)  in subsections (1) and (3) to (5), omit "8(1)";
(b)  in subsection (2), omit "8(1) or"; and
(c)  in subsection (6), for "sections 9, 10 or" substitute "section".

(8) In section 19(3) (restriction on disclosure of information), omit paragraphs (d) and (e).

(9) In section 19(3), after paragraph (q), insert-

"(r) the Competition Act 1998".

(10) In section 19(5)(a), omit "or in anything published under section 4(2)(a) above".

(11) Omit section 22 (which amends the (1973 c. 41.)Fair Trading Act 1973).

(12) In section 24(1) (modifications of provisions about performance of Commission's functions), for from "Part II" to the first "Commission" substitute "Part II of Schedule 7 to the Competition Act 1998 (performance of the Competition Commission's general functions)".

(13) Omit sections 25 to 30 (amendments of the Restrictive Trade Practices Act 1976).

(14) In section 31 (orders and regulations)-

    (a) omit subsection (2); and
    (b) in subsection (3), omit "10".

(15) In section 33 (short title etc)-

    (a) in subsection (2), for "sections 2 to 24" substitute "sections 11 to 13 and sections 15 to 24";
    (b) omit subsections (3) and (4).

### Magistrates' Courts (Northern Ireland) Order 1981 (S.I. 1981/1675 (N.I. 26))

5. In Schedule 6 to the Magistrates' Courts (Northern Ireland) Order 1981, omit paragraphs 42 and 43 (which amend the Restrictive Trade Practices Act 1976).

### Agricultural Marketing (Northern Ireland) Order 1982 (S.I. 1982/1080 (N.I. 12))

6. In Schedule 8 to the Agricultural Marketing (Northern Ireland) Order 1982-

    (a) omit the entry relating to paragraph 16(2) of Schedule 3 to the Fair Trading Act 1973; and
    (b) in the entry relating to the Competition Act 1980-
        (i) for "sections" substitute "section";
        (ii) omit "and 15(3)".

### The Airports Act 1986 (c.31)

7.- (1) The Airports Act 1986 is amended as follows.

(2) In section 44 (which makes provision about references by the CAA to the Competition Commission), for subsection (3) substitute-

"(3) The provisions mentioned in subsection (3A) are to apply in relation to references under this section as if-

    (a) the functions of the Competition Commission in relation to those references were functions under the 1973 Act;
    (b) the expression "merger reference" included a reference under this section;
    (c) in section 70 of the 1973 Act-
        (i) references to the Secretary of State were references to the CAA, and
        (ii) the reference to three months were a reference to six months.

(3A) The provisions are-

(a) sections 70 (time limit for report on merger) and 85 (attendance of witnesses and production of documents) of the 1973 Act;

(b) Part II of Schedule 7 to the Competition Act 1998 (performance of the Competition Commission's general functions); and

(c) section 24 of the 1980 Act (modification of provisions about performance of such functions)."

(3) In section 45, omit subsection (3) (which falls with the repeal of the Restrictive Trade Practices Act 1976).

(4) In section 54 (orders under the 1973 Act or 1980 Act modifying or revoking conditions)-

(a) in subsection (1), omit "or section 10(2)(a) of the 1980 Act";

(b) in subsection (3), omit paragraph (c) and the "or" immediately before it;

(c) in subsection (4), omit "or the 1980 Act".

(5) In section 56 (co-ordination of exercise of functions by CAA and Director General of Fair Trading), in paragraph (a)(ii), omit "or the 1980 Act".

### The Financial Services Act 1986 (c.60)

**8.** In Schedule 11 to the Financial Services Act 1986, in paragraph 12-

(a) in sub-paragraph (1), omit "126";

(b) omit sub-paragraph (2).

### The Companies Consolidation (Consequential Provisions)(Northern Ireland) Order 1986 (S.I. 1986/1035 (N.I. 9))

**9.** In Part II of Schedule 1 to the Companies Consolidation (Consequential Provisions)(Northern Ireland) Order 1986, omit the entries relating to the Restrictive Trade Practices Act 1976 and the Resale Prices Act 1976.

### The Consumer Protection Act 1987 (c.43)

10. In section 38(3) of the Consumer Protection Act 1987 (restrictions on disclosure of information)-

(a) omit paragraphs (e) and (f); and

(b) after paragraph (o), insert-

"(p) the Competition Act 1998."

### The Channel Tunnel Act 1987 (c.53)

**11.** In section 33 of the Channel Tunnel Act 1987-

(a) in subsection (2), omit paragraph (c) and the "and" immediately before it;

(b) in subsection (5), omit paragraphs (b) and (c).

### The Road Traffic (Consequential Provisions) Act 1988 (c.54)

**12.** In Schedule 3 to the Road Traffic (Consequential Provisions) Act 1988 (consequential amendments), omit paragraph 19.

### The Companies Act 1989 (c.40)

**13.** In Schedule 20 to the Companies Act 1989 (amendments about mergers and related matters), omit paragraphs 21 to 24.

### The Broadcasting Act 1990 (c.42)

**14.–** (1) The Broadcasting Act 1990 is amended as follows.

(2) In section 193 (modification of networking arrangements in consequence of reports under competition legislation)-

(a) in subsection (2), omit paragraph (c) and the "and" immediately before it;
(b) in subsection (4), omit "or the Competition Act 1980".

(3) In Schedule 4 (which makes provision for references to the Director or the Competition Commission in respect of networking arrangements), in paragraph 4, for sub-paragraph (7) substitute-

"(7) The provisions mentioned in sub-paragraph (7A) are to apply in relation to references under this paragraph as if-

(a) the functions of the Competition Commission in relation to those references were functions under the Fair Trading Act 1973;
(b) the expression "merger reference" included a reference under this paragraph.

(7A) The provisions are-

(a) section 85 of the Fair Trading Act 1973 (attendance of witnesses and production of documents);
(b) Part II of Schedule 7 to the Competition Act 1998 (performance of the Competition Commission's general functions); and
(c) section 24 of the Competition Act 1980 (modification of provisions about performance of such functions)."

### The Tribunals and Inquiries Act 1992 (c.53)

**15.** In Schedule 1 to the Tribunals and Inquiries Act 1992 (tribunals under the supervision of the Council on Tribunals), after paragraph 9, insert-

"Competition

9A. An appeal tribunal established under section 48 of the Competition Act 1998."

### The Osteopaths Act 1993 (c.21)

**16.** Section 33 of the Osteopaths Act 1993 (competition and anti-competitive practices) is amended as follows-

(a) in subsection (4), omit paragraph (b) and the "or" immediately before it;
(b) in subsection (5), omit "or section 10 of the Act of 1980".

### The Chiropractors Act 1994 (c.17)

**17.** Section 33 of the Chiropractors Act 1994 (competition and anti-competitive practices) is amended as follows-

(a) in subsection (4), omit paragraph (b) and the "or" immediately before it;
(b) in subsection (5), omit "or section 10 of the Act of 1980".

### The Coal Industry Act 1994 (c.21)

**18.** In section 59(4) of the Coal Industry Act 1994 (information to be kept confidential by the Coal Authority)-

(a) omit paragraphs (e) and (f); and
(b) after paragraph (m), insert-

"(n) the Competition Act 1998."

### The Deregulation and Contracting Out Act 1994 (c.40)

**19.–** (1) The Deregulation and Contracting Out Act 1994 is amended as follows.

(2) Omit-

(a) section 10 (restrictive trade practices: non-notifiable agreements); and
(b) section 11 (registration of commercially sensitive information).

(3) In section 12 (anti-competitive practices: competition references), omit subsections (1) to (6).

(4) In Schedule 4, omit paragraph 1.

(5) In Schedule 11 (miscellaneous deregulatory provisions: consequential amendments), in paragraph 4, omit sub-paragraphs (3) to (7).

### The Airports (Northern Ireland) Order 1994 (S.I. 1994/426 (N.I. 1))

**20.–** (1) The Airports (Northern Ireland) Order 1994 is amended as follows.

(2) In Article 35 (which makes provision about references by the CAA to the Competition Commission), for paragraph (3) substitute-

"(3) The provisions mentioned in paragraph (3A) are to apply in relation to references under Article 34 as if-

(a) the functions of the Competition Commission in relation to those references were functions under the 1973 Act;

(b) the expression "merger reference" included a reference under that Article;

(c) in section 70 of the 1973 Act-

(i) references to the Secretary of State were references to the Director, and

(ii) the reference to three months were a reference to six months.

(3A) The provisions are-

(a) sections 70 (time limit for report on merger) and 85 (attendance of witnesses and production of documents) of the 1973 Act;

(b) Part II of Schedule 7 to the Competition Act 1998 (performance of the Competition Commission's general functions); and

(c) section 24 of the 1980 Act (modification of provisions about performance of such functions)."

(3) In Article 36, omit paragraph (3) (which falls with the repeal of the Restrictive Trade Practices Act 1976).

(4) In Article 45 (orders under the 1973 Act or 1980 Act modifying or revoking conditions)-

(a) in paragraph (1), omit "or section 10(2)(a) of the 1980 Act";

(b) in paragraph (3), omit sub-paragraph (c) and the "or" immediately before it;

(c) in paragraph (4), omit "or the 1980 Act".

(5) In Article 47 (co-ordination of exercise of functions by CAA and Director of Fair Trading), in paragraph (a)(ii), omit "or the 1980 Act".

(6) In Schedule 9, omit paragraph 5 (which amends the Restrictive Trade Practices Act 1976).

**The Broadcasting Act 1996 (c.55)**

**21.** In section 77 of the Broadcasting Act 1996 (which modifies the Restrictive Trade Practices Act 1976 in its application to agreements relating to Channel 3 news provision), omit subsection (2).

SCHEDULE 13

TRANSITIONAL PROVISIONS AND SAVINGS

PART I

GENERAL

**Interpretation**

1.– (1) In this Schedule-

"RPA" means the Resale Prices Act 1976;

"RTPA" means the Restrictive Trade Practices Act 1976;

"continuing proceedings" has the meaning given by paragraph 15;

"the Court" means the Restrictive Practices Court;

"Director" means the Director General of Fair Trading;

"document" includes information recorded in any form;

"enactment date" means the date on which this Act is passed;

"information" includes estimates and forecasts;

"interim period" means the period beginning on the enactment date and ending immediately before the starting date;

"prescribed" means prescribed by an order made by the Secretary of State;

"regulator" means any person mentioned in paragraphs (a) to (g) of paragraph 1 of Schedule 10;

"starting date" means the date on which section 2 comes into force;

"transitional period" means the transitional period provided for in Chapters III and IV of Part IV of this Schedule.

(2) Sections 30, 44, 51, 53, 55, 56, 57 and 59(3) and (4) and paragraph 12 of Schedule 9 ("the applied provisions") apply for the purposes of this Schedule as they apply for the purposes of Part I of this Act.

(3) Section 2(5) applies for the purposes of any provisions of this Schedule which are concerned with the operation of the Chapter I prohibition as it applies for the purposes of Part I of this Act.

(4) In relation to any of the matters in respect of which a regulator may exercise powers as a result of paragraph 35(1), the applied provisions are to have effect as if references to the Director included references to the regulator.

(5) The fact that to a limited extent the Chapter I prohibition does not apply to an agreement, because a transitional period is provided by virtue of this Schedule, does not require those provisions of the agreement in respect of which there is a transitional period to be disregarded when considering whether the agreement infringes the prohibition for other reasons.

### General power to make transitional provision and savings

**2.–** (1) Nothing in this Schedule affects the power of the Secretary of State under section 75 to make transitional provisions or savings.

(2) An order under that section may modify any provision made by this Schedule.

### Advice and information

**3.–** (1) The Director may publish advice and information explaining provisions of this Schedule to persons who are likely to be affected by them.

(2) Any advice or information published by the Director under this paragraph is to be published in such form and manner as he considers appropriate.

PART II

DURING THE INTERIM PERIOD

### Block exemptions

**4.–** (1) The Secretary of State may, at any time during the interim period, make one or more orders for the purpose of providing block exemptions which are effective on the starting date.

(2) An order under this paragraph has effect as if properly made under section 6.

### Certain agreements to be non-notifiable agreements

**5.** An agreement which-

(a) is made during the interim period, and
(b) satisfies the conditions set out in paragraphs (a), (c) and (d) of section 27A(1) of the RTPA,

is to be treated as a non-notifiable agreement for the purposes of the RTPA.

### Application of RTPA during the interim period

**6.** In relation to agreements made during the interim period-

(a) the Director is no longer under the duty to take proceedings imposed by section 1(2)(c) of the RTPA but may continue to do so;
(b) section 21 of that Act has effect as if subsections (1) and (2) were omitted; and

    (c) section 35(1) of that Act has effect as if the words "or within such further time as the Director may, upon application made within that time, allow" were omitted.

## Guidance

**7.–** (1) Sub-paragraphs (2) to (4) apply in relation to agreements made during the interim period.

(2) An application may be made to the Director in anticipation of the coming into force of section 13 in accordance with directions given by the Director and such an application is to have effect on and after the starting date as if properly made under section 13.

(3) The Director may, in response to such an application-

    (a) give guidance in anticipation of the coming into force of section 2; or
    (b) on and after the starting date, give guidance under section 15 as if the application had been properly made under section 13.

(4) Any guidance so given is to have effect on and after the starting date as if properly given under section 15.

PART III

ON THE STARTING DATE

## Applications which fall

**8.–** (1) Proceedings in respect of an application which is made to the Court under any of the provisions mentioned in sub-paragraph (2), but which is not determined before the starting date, cease on that date.

(2) The provisions are-

    (a) sections 2(2), 35(3), 37(1) and 40(1) of the RTPA and paragraph 5 of Schedule 4 to that Act;
    (b) section 4(1) of the RTPA so far as the application relates to an order under section 2(2) of that Act; and
    (c) section 25(2) of the RPA.

(3) The power of the Court to make an order for costs in relation to any proceedings is not affected by anything in this paragraph or by the repeals made by section 1.

## Orders and approvals which fall

**9.–** (1) An order in force immediately before the starting date under-

    (a) section 2(2), 29(1), 30(1), 33(4), 35(3) or 37(1) of the RTPA; or
    (b) section 25(2) of the RPA,

ceases to have effect on that date.

(2) An approval in force immediately before the starting date under section 32 of the RTPA ceases to have effect on that date.

PART IV

ON AND AFTER THE STARTING DATE

CHAPTER I

GENERAL

**Duty of Director to maintain register etc.**

**10.**– (1) This paragraph applies even though the relevant provisions of the RTPA are repealed by this Act.

(2) The Director is to continue on and after the starting date to be under the duty imposed by section 1(2)(a) of the RTPA to maintain a register in respect of agreements-

   (a) particulars of which are, on the starting date, entered or filed on the register;
   (b) which fall within sub-paragraph (4);
   (c) which immediately before the starting date are the subject of proceedings under the RTPA which do not cease on that date by virtue of this Schedule; or
   (d) in relation to which a court gives directions to the Director after the starting date in the course of proceedings in which a question arises as to whether an agreement was, before that date-
      (i)  one to which the RTPA applied;
      (ii) subject to registration under that Act;
      (iii) a non-notifiable agreement for the purposes of that Act.

(3) The Director is to continue on and after the starting date to be under the duties imposed by section 1(2)(a) and (b) of the RTPA of compiling a register of agreements and entering or filing certain particulars in the register, but only in respect of agreements of a kind referred to in paragraph (b), (c) or (d) of sub-paragraph (2).

(4) An agreement falls within this sub-paragraph if-

   (a) it is subject to registration under the RTPA but-
      (i)  is not a non-notifiable agreement within the meaning of section 27A of the RTPA, or
      (ii) is not one to which paragraph 5 applies;
   (b) particulars of the agreement have been provided to the Director before the starting date; and
   (c) as at the starting date no entry or filing has been made in the register in respect of the agreement.

(5) Sections 23 and 27 of the RTPA are to apply after the starting date in respect of the register subject to such modifications, if any, as may be prescribed.

(6) In sub-paragraph (2)(d) "court" means-

    (a) the High Court;
    (b) the Court of Appeal;
    (c) the Court of Session;
    (d) the High Court or Court of Appeal in Northern Ireland; or
    (e) the House of Lords.

### RTPA section 3 applications

**11.-** (1) Even though section 3 of the RTPA is repealed by this Act, its provisions (and so far as necessary that Act) are to continue to apply, with such modifications (if any) as may be prescribed-

    (a) in relation to a continuing application under that section; or
    (b) so as to allow an application to be made under that section on or after the starting date in respect of a continuing application under section 1(3) of the RTPA.

(2) "Continuing application" means an application made, but not determined, before the starting date.

### RTPA section 26 applications

**12.-** (1) Even though section 26 of the RTPA is repealed by this Act, its provisions (and so far as necessary that Act) are to continue to apply, with such modifications (if any) as may be prescribed, in relation to an application which is made under that section, but not determined, before the starting date.

(2) If an application under section 26 is determined on or after the starting date, this Schedule has effect in relation to the agreement concerned as if the application had been determined immediately before that date.

### Right to bring civil proceedings

**13.-** (1) Even though section 35 of the RTPA is repealed by this Act, its provisions (and so far as necessary that Act) are to continue to apply in respect of a person who, immediately before the starting date, has a right by virtue of section 27ZA or 35(2) of that Act to bring civil proceedings in respect of an agreement (but only so far as that right relates to any period before the starting date or, where there are continuing proceedings, the determination of the proceedings).

(2) Even though section 25 of the RPA is repealed by this Act, the provisions of that section (and so far as necessary that Act) are to continue to apply in respect of a person who, immediately before the starting date, has a right by virtue of subsection (3) of that section to bring civil proceedings (but only so far as that right relates to any period before the starting date or, where there are continuing proceedings, the determination of the proceedings).

CHAPTER II

CONTINUING PROCEEDINGS

## The general rule

**14.**– (1) The Chapter I prohibition does not apply to an agreement at any time when the agreement is the subject of continuing proceedings under the RTPA.

(2) The Chapter I prohibition does not apply to an agreement relating to goods which are the subject of continuing proceedings under section 16 or 17 of the RPA to the extent to which the agreement consists of exempt provisions.

(3) In sub-paragraph (2) "exempt provisions" means those provisions of the agreement which would, disregarding section 14 of the RPA, be-

(a) void as a result of section 9(1) of the RPA; or
(b) unlawful as a result of section 9(2) or 11 of the RPA.

(4) If the Chapter I prohibition does not apply to an agreement because of this paragraph, the provisions of, or made under, the RTPA or the RPA are to continue to have effect in relation to the agreement.

(5) The repeals made by section 1 do not affect-

(a) continuing proceedings; or
(b) proceedings of the kind referred to in paragraph 11 or 12 of this Schedule which are continuing after the starting date.

## Meaning of "continuing proceedings"

**15.**– (1) For the purposes of this Schedule "continuing proceedings" means proceedings in respect of an application made to the Court under the RTPA or the RPA, but not determined, before the starting date.

(2) But proceedings under section 3 or 26 of the RTPA to which paragraph 11 or 12 applies are not continuing proceedings.

(3) The question whether (for the purposes of Part III, or this Part, of this Schedule) an application has been determined is to be decided in accordance with sub-paragraphs (4) and (5).

(4) If an appeal against the decision on the application is brought, the application is not determined until-

(a) the appeal is disposed of or withdrawn; or
(b) if as a result of the appeal the case is referred back to the Court-
 (i) the expiry of the period within which an appeal ("the further appeal") in respect of the Court's decision on that reference could have been brought had this Act not been passed; or
 (ii) if later, the date on which the further appeal is disposed of or withdrawn.

(5) Otherwise, the application is not determined until the expiry of the period within which any party to the application would have been able to bring an appeal against the decision on the application had this Act not been passed.

## RTPA section 4 proceedings

16. Proceedings on an application for an order under section 4 of the RTPA are also continuing proceedings if-

(a) leave to make the application is applied for before the starting date but the proceedings in respect of that application for leave are not determined before that date; or

(b) leave to make an application for an order under that section is granted before the starting date but the application itself is not made before that date.

## RPA section 16 or 17 proceedings

17. Proceedings on an application for an order under section 16 or 17 of the RPA are also continuing proceedings if-

(a) leave to make the application is applied for before the starting date but the proceedings in respect of that application for leave are not determined before that date; or

(b) leave to make an application for an order under section 16 or 17 of the RPA is granted before the starting date, but the application itself is not made before that date.

## Continuing proceedings which are discontinued

18.– (1) On an application made jointly to the Court by all the parties to any continuing proceedings, the Court must, if it is satisfied that the parties wish it to do so, discontinue the proceedings.

(2) If, on an application under sub-paragraph (1) or for any other reason, the Court orders the proceedings to be discontinued, this Schedule has effect (subject to paragraphs 21 and 22) from the date on which the proceedings are discontinued as if they had never been instituted.

CHAPTER III

THE TRANSITIONAL PERIOD

## The general rule

19.– (1) Except where this Chapter or Chapter IV provides otherwise, there is a transitional period, beginning on the starting date and lasting for one year, for any agreement made before the starting date.

(2) The Chapter I prohibition does not apply to an agreement to the extent to which there is a transitional period for the agreement.

(3) The Secretary of State may by regulations provide for sections 13 to 16 and Schedule 5 to apply with such modifications (if any) as may be specified in the regulations, in respect of applications to the Director about agreements for which there is a transitional period.

**Cases for which there is no transitional period**

**20.**– (1) There is no transitional period for an agreement to the extent to which, immediately before the starting date, it is-

(a) void under section 2(1) or 35(1)(a) of the RTPA;

(b) the subject of an order under section 2(2) or 35(3) of the RTPA; or

(c) unlawful under section 1, 2 or 11 of the RPA or void under section 9 of that Act.

(2) There is no transitional period for an agreement to the extent to which, before the starting date, a person has acted unlawfully for the purposes of section 27ZA(2) or (3) of the RTPA in respect of the agreement.

(3) There is no transitional period for an agreement to which paragraph 25(4) applies.

(4) There is no transitional period for-

(a) an agreement in respect of which there are continuing proceedings, or

(b) an agreement relating to goods in respect of which there are continuing proceedings,

to the extent to which the agreement is, when the proceedings are determined, void or unlawful.

**Continuing proceedings under the RTPA**

**21.** In the case of an agreement which is the subject of continuing proceedings under the RTPA, the transitional period begins-

(a) if the proceedings are discontinued, on the date of discontinuance;

(b) otherwise, when the proceedings are determined.

**Continuing proceedings under the RPA**

**22.**– (1) In the case of an agreement relating to goods which are the subject of continuing proceedings under the RPA, the transitional period for the exempt provisions of the agreement begins-

(a) if the proceedings are discontinued, on the date of discontinuance;

(b) otherwise, when the proceedings are determined.

(2) In sub-paragraph (1) "exempt provisions" has the meaning given by paragraph 14(3).

**Provisions not contrary to public interest**

**23.–** (1) To the extent to which an agreement contains provisions which, immediately before the starting date, are provisions which the Court has found not to be contrary to the public interest, the transitional period lasts for five years.

(2) Sub-paragraph (1) is subject to paragraph 20(4).

(3) To the extent to which an agreement which on the starting date is the subject of continuing proceedings is, when the proceedings are determined, found by the Court not to be contrary to the public interest, the transitional period lasts for five years.

**Goods**

**24.–** (1) In the case of an agreement relating to goods which, immediately before the starting date, are exempt under section 14 of the RPA, there is a transitional period for the agreement to the extent to which it consists of exempt provisions.

(2) Sub-paragraph (1) is subject to paragraph 20(4).

(3) In the case of an agreement relating to goods-

(a) which on the starting date are the subject of continuing proceedings, and
(b) which, when the proceedings are determined, are found to be exempt under section 14 of the RPA,

there is a transitional period for the agreement, to the extent to which it consists of exempt provisions.

(4) In each case, the transitional period lasts for five years.

(5) In sub-paragraphs (1) and (3) "exempt provisions" means those provisions of the agreement which would, disregarding section 14 of the RPA, be-

(a) void as a result of section 9(1) of the RPA; or
(b) unlawful as a result of section 9(2) or 11 of the RPA.

**Transitional period for certain agreements**

**25.–** (1) This paragraph applies to agreements-

(a) which are subject to registration under the RTPA but which-
(i) are not non-notifiable agreements within the meaning of section 27A of the RTPA, or
(ii) are not agreements to which paragraph 5 applies; and
(b) in respect of which the time for furnishing relevant particulars as required by or under the RTPA expires on or after the starting date.

(2) "Relevant particulars" means-

(a) particulars which are required to be furnished by virtue of section 24 of the RTPA; or

(b) particulars of any variation of an agreement which are required to be furnished by virtue of sections 24 and 27 of the RTPA.

(3) There is a transitional period of one year for an agreement to which this paragraph applies if-

(a) relevant particulars are furnished before the starting date; and
(b) no person has acted unlawfully (for the purposes of section 27ZA(2) or (3) of the RTPA) in respect of the agreement.

(4) If relevant particulars are not furnished by the starting date, section 35(1)(a) of the RTPA does not apply in relation to the agreement (unless sub-paragraph (5) applies).

(5) This sub-paragraph applies if a person falling within section 27ZA(2) or (3) of the RTPA has acted unlawfully for the purposes of those subsections in respect of the agreement.

**Special cases**

**26.**– (1) In the case of an agreement in respect of which-

(a) a direction under section 127(2) of the Financial Services Act 1986 ("the 1986 Act") is in force immediately before the starting date, or
(b) a direction under section 194A(3) of the Broadcasting Act 1990 ("the 1990 Act") is in force immediately before the starting date,

the transitional period lasts for five years.

(2) To the extent to which an agreement is the subject of a declaration-

(a) made by the Treasury under section 127(3) of the 1986 Act, and
(b) in force immediately before the starting date,

the transitional period lasts for five years.

(3) Sub-paragraphs (1) and (2) do not affect the power of-

(a) the Treasury to make a declaration under section 127(2) of the 1986 Act (as amended by Schedule 2 to this Act),
(b) the Secretary of State to make a declaration under section 194A of the 1990 Act (as amended by Schedule 2 to this Act),

in respect of an agreement for which there is a transitional period.

CHAPTER IV

THE UTILITIES

**General**

27. In this Chapter "the relevant period" means the period beginning with the starting date and ending immediately before the fifth anniversary of that date.

**Electricity**

28.– (1) For an agreement to which, immediately before the starting date, the RTPA does not apply by virtue of a section 100 order, there is a transitional period-

(a) beginning on the starting date; and
(b) ending at the end of the relevant period.

(2) For an agreement which is made at any time after the starting date and to which, had the RTPA not been repealed, that Act would not at the time at which the agreement is made have applied by virtue of a section 100 order, there is a transitional period-

(a) beginning on the date on which the agreement is made; and
(b) ending at the end of the relevant period.

(3) For an agreement (whether made before or after the starting date) which, during the relevant period, is varied at any time in such a way that it becomes an agreement which, had the RTPA not been repealed, would at that time have been one to which that Act did not apply by virtue of a section 100 order, there is a transitional period-

(a) beginning on the date on which the variation is made; and
(b) ending at the end of the relevant period.

(4) If an agreement for which there is a transitional period as a result of sub-paragraph (1), (2) or (3) is varied during the relevant period, the transitional period for the agreement continues if, had the RTPA not been repealed, the agreement would have continued to be one to which that Act did not apply by virtue of a section 100 order.

(5) But if an agreement for which there is a transitional period as a result of sub-paragraph (1), (2) or (3) ceases to be one to which, had it not been repealed, the RTPA would not have applied by virtue of a section 100 order, the transitional period ends on the date on which the agreement so ceases.

(6) Sub-paragraph (3) is subject to paragraph 20.

(7) In this paragraph and paragraph 29-

"section 100 order" means an order made under section 100 of the Electricity Act 1989; and expressions which are also used in Part I of the Electricity Act 1989 have the same meaning as in that Part.

### Electricity: power to make transitional orders

**29.**– (1) There is a transitional period for an agreement (whether made before or after the starting date) relating to the generation, transmission or supply of electricity which-

   (a) is specified, or is of a description specified, in an order ("a transitional order") made by the Secretary of State (whether before or after the making of the agreement but before the end of the relevant period); and

   (b) satisfies such conditions as may be specified in the order.

(2) A transitional order may make provision as to when the transitional period in respect of such an agreement is to start or to be deemed to have started.

(3) The transitional period for such an agreement ends at the end of the relevant period.

(4) But if the agreement-

   (a) ceases to be one to which a transitional order applies, or

   (b) ceases to satisfy one or more of the conditions specified in the transitional order,

the transitional period ends on the date on which the agreement so ceases.

(5) Before making a transitional order, the Secretary of State must consult the Director General of Electricity Supply and the Director.

(6) The conditions specified in a transitional order may include conditions which refer any matter to the Secretary of State for determination after such consultation as may be so specified.

(7) In the application of this paragraph to Northern Ireland, the reference in sub-paragraph (5) to the Director General of Electricity Supply is to be read as a reference to the Director General of Electricity Supply for Northern Ireland.

### Gas

**30.**– (1) For an agreement to which, immediately before the starting date, the RTPA does not apply by virtue of section 62 or a section 62 order, there is a transitional period-

   (a) beginning on the starting date; and

   (b) ending at the end of the relevant period.

(2) For an agreement which is made at any time after the starting date and to which, had the RTPA not been repealed, that Act would not at the time at which the agreement is made have applied by virtue of section 62 or a section 62 order, there is a transitional period-

(a) beginning on the date on which the agreement is made; and

(b) ending at the end of the relevant period.

(3) For an agreement (whether made before or after the starting date) which, during the relevant period, is varied at any time in such a way that it becomes an agreement which, had the RTPA not been repealed, would at that time have been one to which that Act did not apply by virtue of section 62 or a section 62 order, there is a transitional period-

(a) beginning on the date on which the variation is made; and

(b) ending at the end of the relevant period.

(4) If an agreement for which there is a transitional period as a result of sub-paragraph (1), (2) or (3) is varied during the relevant period, the transitional period for the agreement continues if, had the RTPA not been repealed, the agreement would have continued to be one to which that Act did not apply by virtue of section 62 or a section 62 order.

(5) But if an agreement for which there is a transitional period as a result of sub-paragraph (1), (2) or (3) ceases to be one to which, had it not been repealed, the RTPA would not have applied by virtue of section 62 or a section 62 order, the transitional period ends on the date on which the agreement so ceases.

(6) Sub-paragraph (3) also applies in relation to a modification which is treated as an agreement made on or after 28th November 1985 by virtue of section 62(4).

(7) Sub-paragraph (3) is subject to paragraph 20.

(8) In this paragraph and paragraph 31-

"section 62" means section 62 of the Gas Act 1986;

"section 62 order" means an order made under section 62.

### Gas: power to make transitional orders

31.- (1) There is a transitional period for an agreement of a description falling within section 62(2)(a) and (b) or section 62(2A)(a) and (b) which-

(a) is specified, or is of a description specified, in an order ("a transitional order") made by the Secretary of State (whether before or after the making of the agreement but before the end of the relevant period); and

(b) satisfies such conditions as may be specified in the order.

(2) A transitional order may make provision as to when the transitional period in respect of such an agreement is to start or to be deemed to have started.

(3) The transitional period for such an agreement ends at the end of the relevant period.

(4) But if the agreement-

(a) ceases to be one to which a transitional order applies, or

(b) ceases to satisfy one or more of the conditions specified in the transitional order,

the transitional period ends on the date when the agreement so ceases.

(5) Before making a transitional order, the Secretary of State must consult the Director General of Gas Supply and the Director.

(6) The conditions specified in a transitional order may include-

(a) conditions which are to be satisfied in relation to a time before the coming into force of this paragraph;

(b) conditions which refer any matter (which may be the general question whether the Chapter I prohibition should apply to a particular agreement) to the Secretary of State, the Director or the Director General of Gas Supply for determination after such consultation as may be so specified.

## Gas: Northern Ireland

32.– (1) For an agreement to which, immediately before the starting date, the RTPA does not apply by virtue of an Article 41 order, there is a transitional period-

(a) beginning on the starting date; and
(b) ending at the end of the relevant period.

(2) For an agreement which is made at any time after the starting date and to which, had the RTPA not been repealed, that Act would not at the time at which the agreement is made have applied by virtue of an Article 41 order, there is a transitional period-

(a) beginning on the date on which the agreement is made; and
(b) ending at the end of the relevant period.

(3) For an agreement (whether made before or after the starting date) which, during the relevant period, is varied at any time in such a way that it becomes an agreement which, had the RTPA not been repealed, would at that time have been one to which that Act did not apply by virtue of an Article 41 order, there is a transitional period-

(a) beginning on the date on which the variation is made; and
(b) ending at the end of the relevant period.

(4) If an agreement for which there is a transitional period as a result of sub-paragraph (1), (2) or (3) is varied during the relevant period, the transitional period for the agreement continues if, had the RTPA not been repealed, the agreement would have continued to be one to which that Act did not apply by virtue of an Article 41 order.

(5) But if an agreement for which there is a transitional period as a result of sub-paragraph (1), (2) or (3) ceases to be one to which, had it not been repealed, the RTPA would not have applied by virtue of an Article 41 order, the transitional period ends on the date on which the agreement so ceases.

(6) Sub-paragraph (3) is subject to paragraph 20.

(7) In this paragraph and paragraph 33-

"Article 41 order" means an order under Article 41 of the Gas (Northern Ireland) Order 1996;

"Department" means the Department of Economic Development.

### Gas: Northern Ireland - power to make transitional orders

**33.**– (1) There is a transitional period for an agreement of a description falling within Article 41(1) which-

(a) is specified, or is of a description specified, in an order ("a transitional order") made by the Department (whether before or after the making of the agreement but before the end of the relevant period); and

(b) satisfies such conditions as may be specified in the order.

(2) A transitional order may make provision as to when the transitional period in respect of such an agreement is to start or to be deemed to have started.

(3) The transitional period for such an agreement ends at the end of the relevant period.

(4) But if the agreement-

(a) ceases to be one to which a transitional order applies, or

(b) ceases to satisfy one or more of the conditions specified in the transitional order,

the transitional period ends on the date when the agreement so ceases.

(5) Before making a transitional order, the Department must consult the Director General of Gas for Northern Ireland and the Director.

(6) The conditions specified in a transitional order may include conditions which refer any matter (which may be the general question whether the Chapter I prohibition should apply to a particular agreement) to the Department for determination after such consultation as may be so specified.

### Railways

**34.**– (1) In this paragraph-

"section 131" means section 131 of the Railways Act 1993 ("the 1993 Act");

"section 131 agreement" means an agreement-

(a) to which the RTPA does not apply immediately before the starting date by virtue of section 131(1); or

(b) in respect of which a direction under section 131(3) is in force immediately before that date;

"non-exempt agreement" means an agreement relating to the provision of railway services (whether made before or after the starting date) which is not a section 131 agreement; and

"railway services" has the meaning given by section 82 of the 1993 Act.

(2) For a section 131 agreement there is a transitional period of five years.

(3) There is a transitional period for a non-exempt agreement to the extent to which the agreement is at any time before the end of the relevant period required or approved-

(a) by the Secretary of State or the Rail Regulator in pursuance of any function assigned or transferred to him under or by virtue of any provision of the 1993 Act;

(b) by or under any agreement the making of which is required or approved by the Secretary of State or the Rail Regulator in the exercise of any such function; or

(c) by or under a licence granted under Part I of the 1993 Act.

(4) The transitional period conferred by sub-paragraph (3)-

(a) is to be taken to have begun on the starting date; and

(b) ends at the end of the relevant period.

(5) Sub-paragraph (3) is subject to paragraph 20.

(6) Any variation of a section 131 agreement on or after the starting date is to be treated, for the purposes of this paragraph, as a separate non-exempt agreement.

## The regulators

35.– (1) Subject to sub-paragraph (3), each of the regulators may exercise, in respect of sectoral matters and concurrently with the Director, the functions of the Director under paragraph 3, 7, 19(3), 36, 37, 38 or 39.

(2) In sub-paragraph (1) "sectoral matters" means-

(a) in the case of the Director General of Telecommunications, the matters referred to in section 50(3) of the Telecommunications Act 1984;

(b) in the case of the Director General of Gas Supply, the matters referred to in section 36A(3) and (4) of the Gas Act 1986;

(c) in the case of the Director General of Electricity Supply, the matters referred to in section 43(3) of the Electricity Act 1989;

(d) in the case of the Director General of Electricity Supply for Northern Ireland, the matters referred to in Article 46(3) of the Electricity (Northern Ireland) Order 1992;

(e) in the case of the Director General of Water Services, the matters referred to in section 31(3) of the Water Industry Act 1991;

(f) in the case of the Rail Regulator, the matters referred to in section 67(3) of the Railways Act 1993;

(g) in the case of the Director General of Gas for Northern Ireland, the matters referred to in Article 23(3) of the Gas (Northern Ireland) Order 1996.

(3) The power to give directions in paragraph 7(2) is exercisable by the Director only but if the Director is preparing directions which relate to a matter in respect of which a regulator exercises concurrent jurisdiction, he must consult that regulator.

(4) Consultations conducted by the Director before the enactment date, with a view to preparing directions which have effect on or after that date, are to be taken to satisfy sub-paragraph (3).

(5) References to enactments in sub-paragraph (2) are to the enactments as amended by or under this Act.

## Chapter V

### Extending the transitional period

**36.**– (1) A party to an agreement for which there is a transitional period may apply to the Director, not less than three months before the end of the period, for the period to be extended.

(2) The Director may (on his own initiative or on an application under sub-paragraph (1))-

(a) extend a one-year transitional period by not more than twelve months;
(b) extend a transitional period of any period other than one year by not more than six months.

(3) An application under sub-paragraph (1) must-

(a) be in such form as may be specified; and
(b) include such documents and information as may be specified.

(4) If the Director extends the transitional period under this paragraph, he must give notice in such form, and to such persons, as may be specified.

(5) The Director may not extend a transitional period more than once.

(6) In this paragraph-

"person" has the same meaning as in Part I; and

"specified" means specified in rules made by the Director under section 51.

## CHAPTER VI

## TERMINATING THE TRANSITIONAL PERIOD

### General

**37.** – (1) Subject to sub-paragraph (2), the Director may by a direction in writing terminate the transitional period for an agreement, but only in accordance with paragraph 38.

(2) The Director may not terminate the transitional period, nor exercise any of the powers in paragraph 38, in respect of an agreement which is excluded from the Chapter I prohibition by virtue of any of the provisions of Part I of this Act other than paragraph 1 of Schedule 1 or paragraph 2 or 9 of Schedule 3.

### Circumstances in which the Director may terminate the transitional period

**38.** – (1) If the Director is considering whether to give a direction under paragraph 37 ("a direction"), he may in writing require any party to the agreement concerned to give him such information in connection with that agreement as he may require.

(2) If at the end of such period as may be specified in rules made under section 51, a person has failed, without reasonable excuse, to comply with a requirement imposed under sub-paragraph (1), the Director may give a direction.

(3) The Director may also give a direction if he considers-

    (a) that the agreement would, but for the transitional period or a relevant exclusion, infringe the Chapter I prohibition; and

    (b) that he would not be likely to grant the agreement an unconditional individual exemption.

(4) For the purposes of sub-paragraph (3) an individual exemption is unconditional if no conditions or obligations are imposed in respect of it under section 4(3)(a).

(5) In this paragraph-

"person" has the same meaning as in Part I;

"relevant exclusion" means an exclusion under paragraph 1 of Schedule 1 or paragraph 2 or 9 of Schedule 3.

### Procedural requirements on giving a paragraph 37 direction

**39.** – (1) The Director must specify in a direction under paragraph 37 ("a direction") the date on which it is to have effect (which must not be less than 28 days after the direction is given).

(2) Copies of the direction must be given to-

    (a) each of the parties concerned, and

    (b) the Secretary of State,

not less than 28 days before the date on which the direction is to have effect.

(3) In relation to an agreement to which a direction applies, the transitional period (if it has not already ended) ends on the date specified in the direction unless, before that date, the direction is revoked by the Director or the Secretary of State.

(4) If a direction is revoked, the Director may give a further direction in respect of the same agreement only if he is satisfied that there has been a material change of circumstance since the revocation.

(5) If, as a result of paragraph 24(1) or (3), there is a transitional period in respect of provisions of an agreement relating to goods-

    (a) which immediately before the starting date are exempt under section 14 of the RPA, or

    (b) which, when continuing proceedings are determined, are found to be exempt under section 14 of the RPA,

the period is not affected by paragraph 37 or 38.

## PART V

## THE FAIR TRADING ACT 1973

### References to the Monopolies and Mergers Commission

**40.–** (1) If, on the date on which the repeal by this Act of a provision mentioned in sub-paragraph (2) comes into force, the Monopolies and Mergers Commission has not completed a reference which was made to it before that date, continued consideration of the reference may include consideration of a question which could not have been considered if the provision had not been repealed.

(2) The provisions are-

    (a) sections 10(2), 54(5) and 78(3) and paragraph 3(1) and (2) of Schedule 8 to the Fair Trading Act 1973 (c. 41);

    (b) section 11(8)(b) of the Competition Act 1980 (c. 21);

    (c) section 14(2) of the Telecommunications Act 1984 (c. 12);

    (d) section 45(3) of the Airports Act 1986 (c. 31);

    (e) section 25(2) of the Gas Act 1986 (c. 44);

    (f) section 13(2) of the Electricity Act 1989 (c. 29);

    (g) section 15(2) of the Water Industry Act 1991 (c. 56);

    (h) article 16(2) of the Electricity (Northern Ireland) Order 1992;

    (i) section 14(2) of the Railways Act 1993 (c. 43);

    (j) article 36(3) of the Airports (Northern Ireland) Order 1994;

    (k) article 16(2) of the Gas (Northern Ireland) Order 1996.

### Orders under Schedule 8

**41.–** (1) In this paragraph-

"the 1973 Act" means the Fair Trading Act 1973;

"agreement" means an agreement entered into before the date on which the repeal of the limiting provisions comes into force;

"the order" means an order under section 56 or 73 of the 1973 Act;

"the limiting provisions" means sub-paragraph (1) or (2) of paragraph 3 of Schedule 8 to the 1973 Act (limit on power to make orders under paragraph 1 or 2 of that Schedule) and includes any provision of the order included because of either of those sub-paragraphs; and

"transitional period" means the period which-

(a) begins on the day on which the repeal of the limiting provisions comes into force; and
(b) ends on the first anniversary of the starting date.

(2) Sub-paragraph (3) applies to any agreement to the extent to which it would have been unlawful (in accordance with the provisions of the order) but for the limiting provisions.

(3) As from the end of the transitional period, the order is to have effect in relation to the agreement as if the limiting provisions had never had effect.

## Part III of the Act

42.– (1) The repeals made by section 1 do not affect any proceedings in respect of an application which is made to the Court under Part III of the Fair Trading Act 1973, but is not determined, before the starting date.

(2) The question whether (for the purposes of sub-paragraph (1)) an application has been determined is to be decided in accordance with sub-paragraphs (3) and (4).

(3) If an appeal against the decision on the application is brought, the application is not determined until-

(a) the appeal is disposed of or withdrawn; or
(b) if as a result of the appeal the case is referred back to the Court-
  (i) the expiry of the period within which an appeal ("the further appeal") in respect of the Court's decision on that reference could have been brought had this Act not been passed; or
  (ii) if later, the date on which the further appeal is disposed of or withdrawn.

(4) Otherwise, the application is not determined until the expiry of the period within which any party to the application would have been able to bring an appeal against the decision on the application had this Act not been passed.

(5) Any amendment made by Schedule 12 to this Act which substitutes references to a relevant Court for references to the Court is not to affect proceedings of the kind referred to in sub-paragraph (1).

## PART VI

### THE COMPETITION ACT 1980

**Undertakings**

**43.**– (1) Subject to sub-paragraph (2), an undertaking accepted by the Director under section 4 or 9 of the Competition Act 1980 ceases to have effect on the coming into force of the repeal by this Act of that section.

(2) If the undertaking relates to an agreement which on the starting date is the subject of continuing proceedings, the undertaking continues to have effect for the purposes of section 29 of the Competition Act 1980 until the proceedings are determined.

**Application of sections 25 and 26**

**44.** The repeals made by section 1 do not affect-

(a) the operation of section 25 of the Competition Act 1980 in relation to an application under section 1(3) of the RTPA which is made before the starting date;
(b) an application under section 26 of the Competition Act 1980 which is made before the starting date.

## PART VII

### MISCELLANEOUS

**Disclosure of information**

**45.**– (1) Section 55 of this Act applies in relation to information which, immediately before the starting date, is subject to section 41 of the RTPA as it applies in relation to information obtained under or as a result of Part I.

(2) But section 55 does not apply to any disclosure of information of the kind referred to in sub-paragraph (1) if the disclosure is made-

(a) for the purpose of facilitating the performance of functions of a designated person under the Control of Misleading Advertisements Regulations 1988; or
(b) for the purposes of any proceedings before the Court or of any other legal proceedings under the RTPA or the Fair Trading Act 1973 or the Control of Misleading Advertisements Regulations 1988.

(3) Section 56 applies in relation to information of the kind referred to in sub-paragraph (1) if particulars containing the information have been entered or filed on the special section of the register maintained by the Director under, or as a result of, section 27 of the RTPA or paragraph 10 of this Schedule.

(4) Section 55 has effect, in relation to the matters as to which section 41(2) of the RTPA had effect, as if it contained a provision similar to section 41(2).

**The Court**

**46.** If it appears to the Lord Chancellor that a person who ceases to be a non-judicial member of the Court as a result of this Act should receive compensation for loss of office, he may pay to him out of moneys provided by Parliament such sum as he may with the approval of the Treasury determine.

# SCHEDULE 14

REPEALS

| Chapter | Short title | Extent of repeal |
| --- | --- | --- |
| 1973 c. 41. | The Fair Trading Act 1973. | Section 4.<br>Section 10(2).<br>Section 45.<br>Section 54(5).<br>Section 78(3).<br>In section 81(1), in the words before paragraph (a), from "and the Commission" to "of this Act)"; in paragraph (b), "or the Commission, as the case may be" and "or of the Commission"; in subsection (2), "or the Commission" and "or of the Commission" and in subsection (3), from "and, in the case," to "85 of this Act", and "or the Commission, as the case may be,".<br>In section 83, in subsection (1) "Subject to subsection (1A) below" and subsection (1A).<br>In section 135(1), in the words before paragraph (a) and in paragraph (b), "or the Commission", and paragraph (a).<br>Schedule 3.<br>In Schedule 8, paragraph 3(1) and (2). |
| 1976 c. 33. | The Restrictive Practices Court Act 1976. | The whole Act. |
| 1976 c. 34. | The Restrictive Trade Practices Act 1976. | The whole Act. |
| 1976 c. 53. | The Resale Prices Act 1976. | The whole Act. |
| 1976 c. 76. | The Energy Act 1976. | Section 5. |
| 1977 c. 19. | The Restrictive Trade Practices Act 1977. | The whole Act. |

| Chapter | Short title | Extent of repeal |
| --- | --- | --- |
| 1977 c. 37. | The Patents Act 1977. | Sections 44 and 45. |
| 1979 c. 38. | The Estate Agents Act 1979. | In section 10(3), "or the Restrictive Trade Practices Act 1976." |
| 1980 c. 21. | The Competition Act 1980. | Sections 2 to 10.<br>In section 11(8), paragraph (b) and the "and" immediately before it.<br>In section 13(1), from "but the giving" to the end.<br>In section 15, subsections (2)(b), (3) and (4).<br>Section 16(3).<br>In section 17, "8(1)" in subsections (1) and (3) to (5) and in subsection (2) "8(1) or".<br>In section 19(3), paragraph (d).<br>In section 19(5)(a), "or in anything published under section 4(2)(a) above".<br>Section 22.<br>Sections 25 to 30.<br>In section 31, subsection (2) and "10" in subsection (3).<br>Section 33(3) and (4). |
| 1984 c. 12. | The Telecommunications Act 1984. | Section 14(2).<br>In section 16(5), the "or" immediately after paragraph (a).<br>In section 50(4), paragraph (c) and the "and" immediately after it.<br>In section 50(5), "or (3)".<br>In section 50(7), "or the 1980 Act".<br>In section 95(1), "or section 10(2)(a) of the 1980 Act".<br>In section 95(2), paragraph (c) and the "or" immediately before it. |

| Chapter | Short title | Extent of repeal |
|---|---|---|
| 1984 c. 12.<br>– *contd.* | The Telecommunications Act 1984. – *contd.* | In section 95(3), "or the 1980 Act".<br>In section 101(3), paragraphs (d) and (e). |
| 1986 c. 31. | The Airports Act 1986. | Section 45(3).<br>In section 54(1), "or section 10(2)(a) of the 1980 Act".<br>In section 54(3), paragraph (c) and the "or" immediately before it.<br>In section 54(4), "or the 1980 Act".<br>In section 56(a)(ii), "or the 1980 Act". |
| 1986 c. 44. | The Gas Act 1986. | Section 25(2).<br>In section 27(1), "or section 10(2)(a) of the Competition Act 1980".<br>In section 27(3)(a), from "or" to "competition reference".<br>In section 27(6), "or the said Act of 1980".<br>In section 28(5), the "or" immediately after paragraph (aa).<br>In section 36A(5), paragraph (d) and the "and" immediately before it.<br>In section 36A(6), "or (3)".<br>In section 36A(8), "or under the 1980 Act".<br>In section 36A(9), "or the 1980 Act".<br>In section 42(3), paragraphs (e) and (f). |
| 1986 c. 60. | The Financial Services Act 1986. | Section 126. |
| 1987 c. 43. | The Consumer Protection Act 1987. | In section 38(3), paragraphs (e) and (f). |

| Chapter | Short title | Extent of repeal |
|---|---|---|
| 1987 c. 53. | The Channel Tunnel Act 1987. | In section 33(2), paragraph (c) and the "and" immediately before it.<br>In section 33(5), paragraphs (b) and (c). |
| 1988 c. 54. | The Road Traffic (Consequential Provisions) Act 1988. | In Schedule 3, paragraph 19. |
| 1989 c. 15. | The Water Act 1989. | In section 174(3), paragraphs (d) and (e). |
| 1989 c. 29. | The Electricity Act 1989. | Section 13(2).<br>In section 15(1), paragraph (b) and the "or" immediately before it.<br>In section 15(2), paragraph (c) and the "or" immediately before it.<br>In section 15(3), "or the 1980 Act".<br>In section 25(5), the "or" immediately after paragraph (b).<br>In section 43(4), paragraph (c) and the "and" immediately after it.<br>In section 43(5), "or (3)".<br>In section 43(7), "or the 1980 Act".<br>In section 57(3), paragraphs (d) and (e). |
| 1989 c. 40. | The Companies Act 1989. | In Schedule 20, paragraphs 21 to 24. |
| 1990 c. 42. | The Broadcasting Act 1990. | In section 193(2), paragraph (c) and the "and" immediately before it.<br>In section 193(4), "or the Competition Act 1980". |
| 1991 c. 56. | The Water Industry Act 1991. | In section 12(5), "or the 1980 Act".<br>Section 15(2). |

| Chapter | Short title | Extent of repeal |
|---|---|---|
| 1991 c. 56.<br>– *contd.* | The Water Industry Act 1991. – *contd.* | In section 17(1), paragraph (b) and the "or" immediately before it.<br>In section 17(2), paragraph (c) and the "or" immediately before it.<br>In section 17(4), "or the 1980 Act".<br>In section 31(4), paragraph (c) and the "and" immediately before it.<br>In section 31(5), "or in subsection (3) above".<br>In section 31(6), "or in subsection (3) above".<br>In section 31(7), "or (3)".<br>In section 31(9), "or the 1980 Act".<br>In Part II of Schedule 15, the entries relating to the Restrictive Trade Practices Act 1976 and the Resale Prices Act 1976. |
| 1991 c. 57. | The Water Resources Act 1991. | In Part II of Schedule 24, the entries relating to the Restrictive Trade Practices Act 1976 and the Resale Prices Act 1976. |
| 1993 c. 21. | The Osteopaths Act 1993. | In section 33(4), paragraph (b) and the "or" immediately before it.<br>In section 33(5), "or section 10 of the Act of 1980". |
| 1993 c. 43. | The Railways Act 1993. | Section 14(2).<br>In section 16(1), paragraph (b) and the "or" immediately before it.<br>In section 16(2), paragraph (c) and the "or" immediately before it.<br>In section 16(5), "or the 1980 Act". |

| Chapter | Short title | Extent of repeal |
|---|---|---|
| 1993 c. 43.<br>– *contd.* | The Railways Act 1993.<br>– *contd.* | In section 67(4), paragraph (c) and the "and" immediately after it.<br>In section 67(6)(a), "or (3)".<br>In section 67(9), "or under the 1980 Act".<br>Section 131.<br>In section 145(3), paragraphs (d) and (e). |
| 1994 c. 17. | The Chiropractors Act 1994. | In section 33(4), paragraph (b) and the "or" immediately before it.<br>In section 33(5), "or section 10 of the Act of 1980". |
| 1994 c. 21. | The Coal Industry Act 1994. | In section 59(4), paragraphs (e) and (f). |
| 1994 c. 40. | The Deregulation and Contracting Out Act 1994. | Sections 10 and 11.<br>In section 12, subsections (1) to (6).<br>In Schedule 4, paragraph 1.<br>In Schedule 11, in paragraph 4, sub-paragraphs (3) to (6). |
| 1996 c. 55. | The Broadcasting Act 1996. | Section 77(2). |

PART II

REVOCATIONS

| Reference | Title | Extent of revocation |
|---|---|---|
| S.I. 1981/1675 (N.I.26). | The Magistrates' Courts (Northern Ireland) Order 1981. | In Schedule 6, paragraphs 42 and 43. |
| S.I. 1982/1080 (N.I.12). | The Agricultural Marketing (Northern Ireland) Order 1982. | In Schedule 8, the entry relating to paragraph 16(2) of Schedule 3 to the Fair Trading Act 1973 and in the entry relating to the Competition Act 1980, "and 15(3)". |

| Reference | Title | Extent of revocation |
|---|---|---|
| S.I. 1986/1035 (N.I.9). | The Companies Consolidation (Consequential Provisions) (Northern Ireland) Order 1986. | In Part II of Schedule 1, the entries relating to the Restrictive Trade Practices Act 1976 and the Resale Prices Act 1976. |
| S.I. 1992/231 (N.I.1). | The Electricity (Northern Ireland) Order 1992. | Article 16(2).<br>In Article 18-<br>  (a) in paragraph (1), sub-paragraph (b) and the "or" immediately before it;<br>  (b) in paragraph (2), sub-paragraph (c) and the "or" immediately before it;<br>  (c) in paragraph (3) "or the 1980 Act".<br>In Article 28(5), the "or" immediately after sub-paragraph (b).<br>In Article 46-<br>  (a) in paragraph (4), sub-paragraph (c) and the "and" immediately after it;<br>  (b) in paragraph (5), "or (3)";<br>  (c) in paragraph (7), "or the 1980 Act".<br>Article 61(3)(f) and (g).<br>In Schedule 12, paragraph 16. |
| S.I. 1994/426 (N.I.1). | The Airports (Northern Ireland) Order 1994. | Article 36(3).<br>In Article 45-<br>  (a) in paragraph (1), "or section 10(2)(a) of the 1980 Act";<br>  (b) in paragraph (3), sub-paragraph (c) and the "or" immediately before it;<br>  (c) in paragraph (4), "or the 1980 Act".<br>In Article 47(a)(ii), "or the 1980 Act".<br>In Schedule 9, paragraph 5. |

| Reference | Title | Extent of revocation |
|---|---|---|
| S.I. 1996/275 (N.I.2). | The Gas (Northern Ireland) Order 1996. | Article 16(2).<br>In Article 18-<br>  (a) in paragraph (1), sub-paragraph (b) and the "or" immediately before it;<br>  (b) in paragraph (3), sub-paragraph (c) and the "or" immediately before it;<br>  (c) in paragraph (5), "or the 1980 Act".<br>In Article 19(5), the "or" immediately after sub-paragraph (b).<br>In Article 23-<br>  (a) in paragraph (4), sub-paragraph (d) and the "and" immediately before it;<br>  (b) in paragraph (5), "or (3)";<br>  (c) in paragraph (7), "or under the 1980 Act";<br>  (d) in paragraph (8), "or the 1980 Act".<br>Article 44(4)(f) and (g). |

# Index

provisional decisions
  Director General's rules 121
  investigations 102–103
provisions, not contrary to public
    interest 162
public interest
  information disclosure 62–63
  provisions not contrary to 162
public policy, exclusions 95–96
publication, decisions 103, 105
publishing information, prohibitions
    58–59
purchase imposition 28

Rail Regulator 124, 129–130, 139–140
railways, transitional provisions 168–169
Railways Act 1993 124, 129–130, 139–140
re-opening files, Director General 31
reasonable assumption
  defence 45
  immunity 45
reasonable grounds, suspecting
    infringement 34–35, 44
reform of legislation 1
register maintenance 157–158
Registrar of Appeal Tribunals 117, 120
Regulating provisions, definition 84, 94
Regulations
  *see also* rules
  agreements 17–18
  definitions 17, 19
  provision 75–76
  Secretary of State 19
  transitional provisions 19
Regulators 59–60, 124–143
  definition 59
  The Prohibitions 124–132
  transitional provisions 169–170
  utilities 132–141
relevant court, definition 145
relevant decisions, appeals 54
relevant functions
  confidentiality 62
  definition 144
relevant party, definition 64

relevant product market 26
religious services 101
removal from list, professional rules 99
remuneration, Competition Commission
    108–109
repeals 78, 176–181
replacement, member of group 111
reporting panel members
  definitions 106
  Monopolies and Mergers Commission
    115
Resale Prices Act 1976 3, 135, 136, 154
  gas 142–143
  water 138
response to appeals 118
responsibility obligations, producers
    91–92
restriction
  agreement benefits 17
  prohibition 5–6
Restrictive Practices Court Act 1976 3
Restrictive Trade Practices Act 1976 1, 3,
    9, 89, 91, 92, 154
  continuing proceedings 160
  electricity 136
  gas 135, 142–143
  interim periods 155–156
  railways 139, 140
  starting dates applications 158
  telecommunications 133
  water 137, 138
Restrictive Trade Practices Act 1977 3
reviewing the list, professional rules
    98–99
reviews, pre-hearing 118
revocation of Acts 181–183
Road Traffic (Consequential Provisions)
    Act 1988 151
RPA *see* Resale Prices Act 1976
RTPA *see* Restrictive Trade Practices Act
    1976
rules
  *see also* professional rules; Regulations
  applications 102, 104
  definitions 59, 102, 104

195

Index compiled by George Curzon,
*Indexing Specialists*, Hove.